FreeSpirit
Block Party

40 QUILT BLOCKS
5 SAMPLERS
20 MODERN DESIGNERS

FreeSpirit Fabrics

stashBOOKS®

an imprint of C&T Publishing

Text copyright © 2018 by FreeSpirit Fabrics

Photography and artwork copyright © 2018 by C&T Publishing, Inc.

PUBLISHER: Amy Marson

CREATIVE DIRECTOR: Gailen Runge

ACQUISITIONS EDITOR: Roxane Cerda

MANAGING EDITOR: Liz Aneloski

EDITORIAL COMPILERS: Nancy Jewell and Lindsay Conner

EDITOR: Karla Menaugh

TECHNICAL EDITOR: Helen Frost

COVER/BOOK DESIGNER: April Mostek

PRODUCTION COORDINATOR: Zinnia Heinzmann

PRODUCTION EDITOR: Alice Mace Nakanishi

ILLUSTRATOR: Kirstie L. Pettersen

PHOTO ASSISTANT: Mai Yong Vang

COVER PHOTOGRAPHY by Lucy Glover

STYLE PHOTOGRAPHY by Lucy Glover and INSTRUCTIONAL PHOTOGRAPHY by Mai Yong Vang of C&T Publishing, Inc., unless otherwise noted

Published by Stash Books, an imprint of C&T Publishing, Inc., P.O. Box 1456, Lafayette, CA 94549

Library of Congress Cataloging-in-Publication Data

Names: FreeSpirit Fabrics.

Title: FreeSpirit block party : 40 quilt blocks, 5 samplers, 20 modern designers / FreeSpirit Fabrics.

Description: Lafayette, CA : Stash Books, an imprint of C&T Publishing, Inc., 2018.

Identifiers: LCCN 2018003528 | ISBN 9781617456886 (soft cover)

Subjects: LCSH: Patchwork--Patterns. | Quilting--Patterns.

Classification: LCC TT835 .F745 2018 | DDC 746.46/041--dc23

LC record available at https://lccn.loc.gov/2018003528

Printed in China

10 9 8 7 6 5 4 3 2

Dedication

This book is dedicated to Project Night Night (projectnightnight.org), a nonprofit organization making a world of difference in the lives of homeless children. We are heartened by the group's mission to supply care packages to youth—including a new canvas tote bag, a blanket to snuggle in, a book, and a stuffed animal to cuddle. All proceeds from the sale of this book will go toward Project Night Night's fund, to help them meet their goal of supplying care packages to every child who needs one.

With Love,

—*Nancy Jewell*,
   on behalf of FreeSpirit Fabrics
   #freespiritfabrics

Acknowledgments

To the many designers, quilters, and dreamers who've put their creative touch on this project, thank you. It takes so many people to write a book, including those who are careful with every last detail, spending hours tweaking the patterns. As always, thank you to our book team at C&T: Karla, Helen, Alice, Zinnia, Lucy, Mai, and April, and also Kerri Thomson for technical writing. My warmest thanks go to Roxane Cerda and Nancy Jewell for inviting me into this collaboration. Sewing quilts on a deadline is no easy task, and I couldn't have done it without support from Baby Lock sewing machines, Coats, and Quilter's Dream batting.

Happy quilting,

—*Lindsay Conner*

Part 1: Sampler Blocks

HEATHER BAILEY

Boutonniere, 8

Solitaire, 9

AMY BUTLER

Coronet, 11

Diadem, 14

Revolution, 17

DENA DESIGNS

Corsage, 20

JOEL DEWBERRY

Arizona, 21

On Target, 23

Sunset, 26

KATHY DOUGHTY

Star Popper, 27

Value Matters, 28

MARGOT ELENA

Spun, 31

LAURA HEINE

Collage Basket, 32

ANNA MARIA HORNER

Melon Flower, 34

KAFFE FASSETT COLLECTIVE

Kaleidoscope, 36

ERIN MCMORRIS

Askew, 38

Spooled, 40

VERNA MOSQUERA

Orange Peel, 42

Snowy Owl, 45

SHANNON NEWLIN

Agape, 48

London, 52

JENNIFER PAGANELLI

Judith's Fan, 55

Sunny Isle Butterflies, 59

TULA PINK

Fly Away, 62

Tidepool, 63

Wildwood, 64

AMY REBER

Mod Cabin, 65

Spinwheel, 68

JANE SASSAMAN ————————

Derailed, 70   Maltese, 71

DENYSE SCHMIDT ————————

Five Spot, 73   Snowbank, 76   X Marks the Spot, 77

SNOW LEOPARD DESIGNS ————————

Four Points, 79   Sunburst, 81

SHARON THORNTON ————————

Compass, 84   Prismatic, 86   Windblown, 88

TANYA WHELAN ————————

Glamping, 90   Six Sides, 92

Part 2 : Sampler Quilts

OVER HERE, 96
9 blocks,
beginner

SUBDIVISION, 100
15 blocks,
beginner

TRIBAL, 104
6 blocks,
advanced beginner

COZY, 108
4 blocks,
intermediate

NEIGHBORS, 114
9 blocks,
intermediate

Quiltmaking Techniques   119
Half-square triangles • Triangle corners • Flying Geese
Foundation paper piecing • Needle-turn appliqué

About the Designers   122

About the Compilers   127

Introduction

When you have 20 fabulous fabric designers, 40 blocks, 5 quilts … there are endless possibilities! Taking a modern spin on the classics, FreeSpirit Fabrics and its talented portfolio of fabric designers share 40 mix-and-match block ideas for sampler quilts. The blocks were compiled by FreeSpirit marketing director Nancy Jewell and experienced quilter and author Lindsay Conner, who then turned the blocks into modern sampler quilts.

In **PART 1** (next page), you'll learn how to assemble each 12″ finished block using techniques from basic patchwork to appliqué or foundation paper-piecing. Each block is the interpretation of a traditional block by a FreeSpirit designer in their own fabrics, with plenty of illustrations to help you piece them to perfection. The patterns are printed in the book *and* available online as PDFs that you may download and print:

tinyurl.com/11314-patterns-download

In **PART 2** (page 95), you'll have fun putting the blocks together into sampler quilts. Whether you're up for a lap quilt like *Cozy* (page 108) or double-size *Neighbors* (page 114), these five projects will give you some out-of-the-box ideas for showing off your blocks with a modern twist, all made even lovelier with beautiful quilting.

Part 1: Sampler Blocks

Taking their inspiration from classic quilt blocks—such as the Log Cabin, Orange Peel, and Windmill—fabric designers are sharing with you their new favorites on the pages that follow.

All blocks are 12″ squares finished (check the measurements; they should be 12½″ squares with seam allowances; trim as needed) so you can mix and match them in the five sampler quilt projects (page 95).

Tips for Success:

- Use a new needle and high-quality thread in your sewing machine. We used Coats all-purpose quilting cotton thread for creating our blocks and quilts.

- Check your machine's tension before you start to sew, and use a ¼″ foot to sew a scant ¼″ seam. One tip for getting the right measurement is to use a seam guide (such as C&T's Sewing Edge—Reusable Vinyl Stops for Your Machine) in front of the presser foot.

- Measure twice, cut once! Use a new rotary cutter blade for the most accurate cuts.

- Pressing matters! The block instructions refer to Quiltmaking Techniques (page 119) for pressing basic units, such as triangle corners, square-in-a-square, snowball, and Flying Geese. The pressing for other units is shown with arrows on the illustrations.

- When you don't have time to make a whole quilt, make a block!

Boutonniere

**FINISHED BLOCK:
12″ × 12″**

Block designed by Heather Bailey, sewn by Kerri Thomson

Fabric collection: FreeSpirit Hello Love by Heather Bailey

Technique: Piecing

See this block in *Over Here* (page 96).

Ingredients

BLUE PRINT: ⅛ yard

CREAM PRINT: ⅛ yard

PINK PRINT: 1 rectangle 3½″ × 12½″

GOLD SOLID: 1 rectangle 3½″ × 12½″

FLORAL: 1 rectangle 3½″ × 12½″

Cutting

BLUE PRINT

• Cut 8 squares 2⅞″ × 2⅞″.

• Cut 4 squares 2½″ × 2½″.

CREAM PRINT

• Cut 12 squares 2⅞″ × 2⅞″.

PINK PRINT, GOLD SOLID, AND FLORAL PRINT

• *From each:* Cut 4 squares 2⅞″ × 2⅞″.

Construction

Note: All seam allowances are a scant ¼″.
See arrows on the illustrations for pressing direction.

1 | Using the 2⅞″ squares, make 8 half-square triangles (page 119) in each of the following color combinations.

• 8 blue/gold • 8 blue/cream
• 8 pink/cream • 8 floral/cream

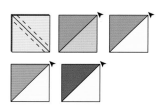

2 | Assemble the block as shown.

Block assembly

Solitaire

FINISHED BLOCK: 12″ × 12″

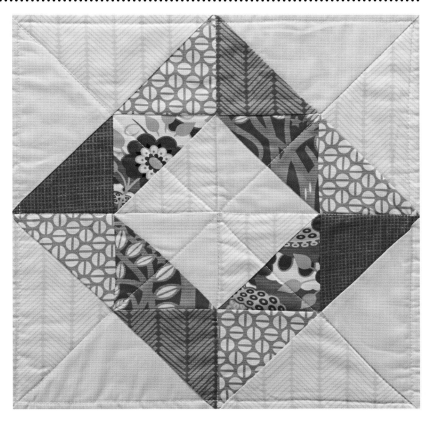

Block designed by Heather Bailey, sewn by Kerri Thomson

Fabric collections: FreeSpirit Hello Love and True Colors by Heather Bailey

Technique: Piecing

See this block in *Cozy* (page 108).

Ingredients

CREAM PRINTS: 2 fat eighths of different prints

RED PRINTS: 4 squares 5″ × 5″ of different prints

ORANGE PRINT: 1 rectangle 5″ × 10″

Cutting

CREAM PRINTS

From each print:

- Cut 1 square 7¼″ × 7¼″.
  Subcut in half diagonally twice.

- Cut 1 square 3⅞″ × 3⅞″.
  Subcut in half diagonally once.

RED PRINTS

From each print:

- Cut 1 square 3⅞″ × 3⅞″.
  Subcut in half diagonally once.

ORANGE PRINT

- Cut 2 squares 3⅞″ × 3⅞″.
  Subcut in half diagonally once.

Construction

Note: All seam allowances are a scant ¼˝. See arrows on the illustrations for pressing direction.

1 | Sew the large triangles together in pairs. Make 4.

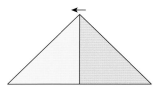

2 | Sew the small red and cream triangles together to make 4 half-square triangle blocks.

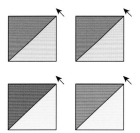

3 | Sew a small orange triangle and a small red triangle to each red edge of the half-square triangles. Make 4.

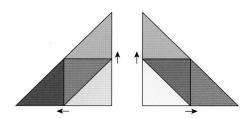

4 | Sew the units from Steps 1 and 3 together. Make 4.

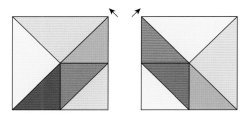

5 | Assemble the block as shown.

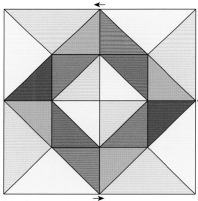

Block assembly

Coronet

FINISHED BLOCK:
12˝ × 12˝

Block designed by Stacey Day with
Amy Butler, sewn by Stacey Day

Fabric collection: FreeSpirit Soul Mate
by Amy Butler

Technique: Foundation paper piecing

See this block in *Over Here* (page 96).

Ingredients

IVORY PRINT: ⅛ yard

AQUA PRINT: ⅛ yard

NAVY PRINT: ⅛ yard

CORAL PRINT: ⅛ yard

CORONET FOUNDATION
PATTERNS A AND B (page 13):
Make 4 copies of each pattern.
(To download, see page 6.)

Cutting

See the pattern (page 13) for piece labels.

IVORY PRINT
- Cut 2 squares 4˝ × 4˝.
  Subcut in half diagonally
  once (4B).
- Cut 2 squares 3⅛˝ × 3⅛˝.
  Subcut in half diagonally
  once (5B).
- Cut 4 rectangles 3¼˝ × 4˝ (1A).

AQUA PRINT
- Cut 2 squares 4˝ × 4˝.
  Subcut in half diagonally
  once (4A).
- Cut 2 squares 3⅛˝ × 3⅛˝.
  Subcut in half diagonally
  once (5A).
- Cut 4 rectangles 3¼˝ × 4˝ (1B).

NAVY PRINT
- Cut 8 rectangles 2¼˝ × 3⅛˝
  (2A and 2B).

CORAL PRINT
- Cut 8 rectangles 2˝ × 2¼˝
  (3A and 3B).

Construction

Note: All seam allowances are a scant ¼˝. Press each seam as it is sewn, using a dry iron.

1 | Refer to Foundation Paper Piecing (page 120) to piece the A and B foundations in order, matching the fabric to the sections listed on the paper. Make 4 each of A and B.

2 | Trim the foundation triangles on the outside solid line. Remove the papers in reverse order.

3 | Sew each foundation A triangle to a foundation B triangle. Make 4.

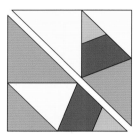

4 | Assemble the block as shown.

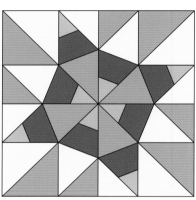

Block assembly

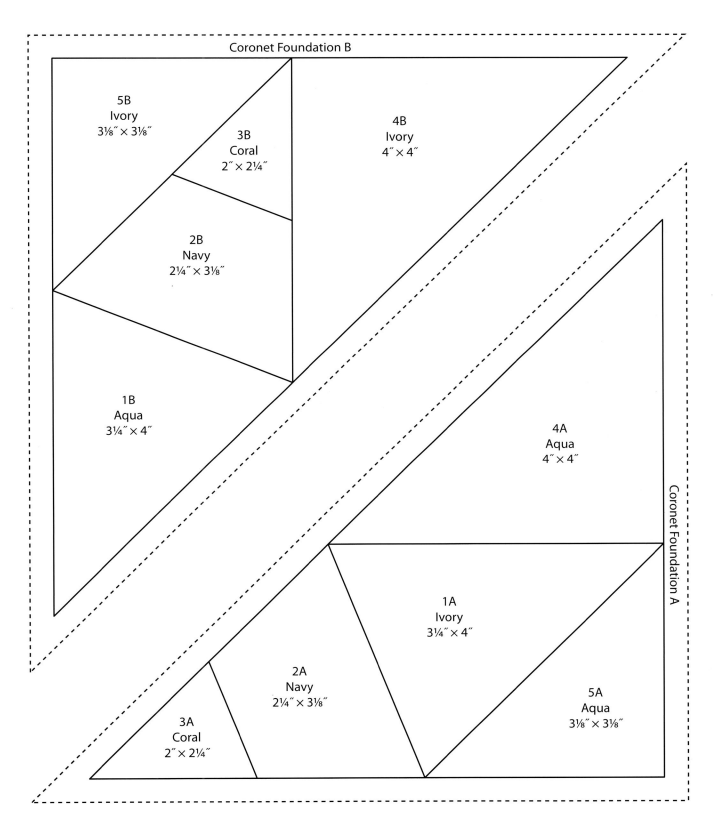

Coronet Foundation B

5B
Ivory
3⅛″ × 3⅛″

3B
Coral
2″ × 2¼″

4B
Ivory
4″ × 4″

2B
Navy
2¼″ × 3⅛″

1B
Aqua
3¼″ × 4″

4A
Aqua
4″ × 4″

Coronet Foundation A

1A
Ivory
3¼″ × 4″

2A
Navy
2¼″ × 3⅛″

3A
Coral
2″ × 2¼″

5A
Aqua
3⅛″ × 3⅛″

Diadem

FINISHED BLOCK:
12″ × 12″

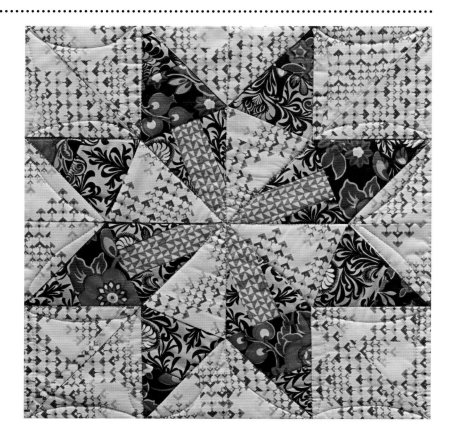

Block designed by Stacey Day with Amy Butler, sewn by Stacey Day

Fabric collection: FreeSpirit Soul Mate by Amy Butler

Technique: Foundation paper piecing

See this block in *Over Here* (page 96).

Ingredients

IVORY PRINT: ⅛ yard

AQUA PRINT: ⅛ yard

NAVY PRINT: ⅛ yard

CORAL PRINT: ⅛ yard

DIADEM FOUNDATION PATTERNS A AND B (page 16): Make 4 copies of each pattern. (To download, see page 6.)

Cutting

See the pattern (page 16) for piece labels.

IVORY PRINT
- Cut 4 squares 4″ × 4″. Subcut in half diagonally once (4A and 6B).
- Cut 4 squares 3⅛″ × 3⅛″. Subcut in half diagonally once (5A and 7B).
- Cut 4 rectangles 3¼″ × 4″ (3A).

AQUA PRINT
- Cut 4 rectangles 2¼″ × 3⅛″ (1A).
- Cut 4 rectangles 2″ × 2¼″ (5B).
- Cut 8 rectangles 1½″ × 3½″ (2B and 3B).

NAVY PRINT
- Cut 4 rectangles 2¼″ × 3⅛″ (4B).
- Cut 4 rectangles 2″ × 2¼″ (2A).

CORAL PRINT
- Cut 4 rectangles 1½″ × 4″ (1B).

Construction

Note: All seam allowances are a scant ¼˝. Press each seam as it is sewn, using a dry iron.

1 | Refer to Foundation Paper Piecing (page 120) to piece the A and B foundations in order, matching the fabric to the sections listed on the paper. Make 4 each of A and B.

2 | Trim the foundation triangles on the outside solid line. Remove the papers in reverse order.

3 | Sew each foundation A triangle to a foundation B triangle. Make 4.

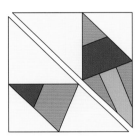

4 | Assemble the block as shown.

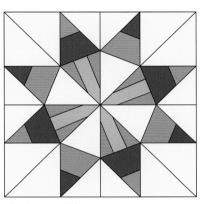

Block assembly

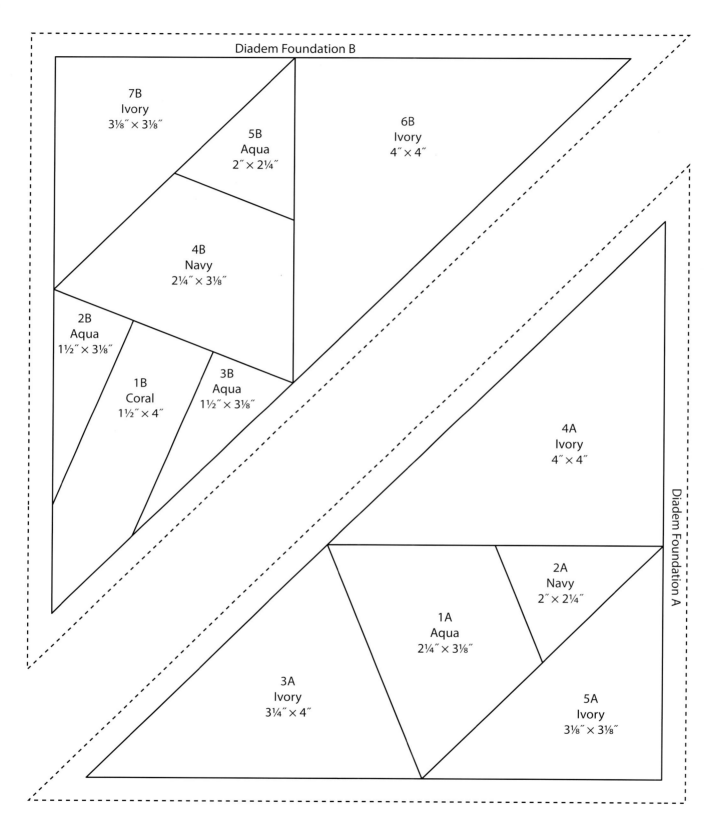

Diadem Foundation B

7B
Ivory
3⅛″ × 3⅛″

5B
Aqua
2″ × 2¼″

6B
Ivory
4″ × 4″

4B
Navy
2¼″ × 3⅛″

2B
Aqua
1½″ × 3⅛″

1B
Coral
1½″ × 4″

3B
Aqua
1½″ × 3⅛″

4A
Ivory
4″ × 4″

2A
Navy
2″ × 2¼″

1A
Aqua
2¼″ × 3⅛″

5A
Ivory
3⅛″ × 3⅛″

3A
Ivory
3¼″ × 4″

Diadem Foundation A

Revolution

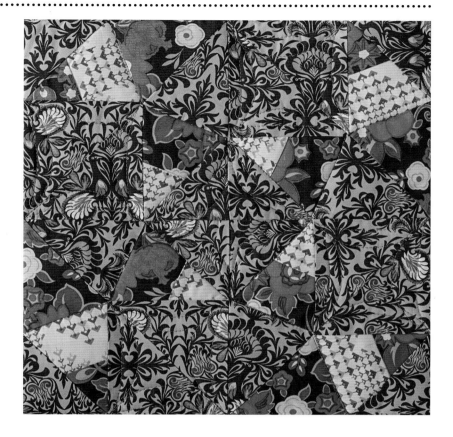

Block designed by Stacey Day with Amy Butler, sewn by Stacey Day

---

Fabric collection: FreeSpirit Soul Mate by Amy Butler

Technique: Foundation paper piecing

See this block in *Neighbors* (page 114).

Ingredients

IVORY PRINT: ⅛ yard

AQUA PRINT: ⅛ yard

NAVY PRINT: ⅛ yard

REVOLUTION FOUNDATION PATTERNS A AND B (page 19):
Make 4 copies of each pattern. (To download, see page 6.)

Cutting

See the pattern (page 19) for piece labels.

IVORY PRINT

- Cut 4 rectangles 2¼″ × 3⅛″ (2B).
- Cut 4 rectangles 2″ × 2¼″ (2A).

AQUA PRINT

- Cut 4 squares 4″ × 4″. Subcut in half diagonally once (4A and 4B).
- Cut 4 squares 3⅛″ × 3⅛″. Subcut in half diagonally once (5A and 5B).
- Cut 4 rectangles 3¼″ × 4″ (3A).

NAVY PRINT

- Cut 4 rectangles 2¼″ × 3⅛″ (1A).
- Cut 4 rectangles 2″ × 2¼″ (3B).
- Cut 4 rectangles 3¼″ × 4″ (1B).

Construction

Note: All seam allowances are a scant ¼˝. Press each seam as it is sewn, using a dry iron.

1 | Refer to Foundation Paper Piecing (page 120) to piece the A and B foundations in order, matching the fabric to the sections listed on the paper. Make 4 each of A and B.

2 | Trim the foundation triangles on the outside solid line. Remove the papers in reverse order.

3 | Sew each foundation A triangle to a foundation B triangle. Make 4.

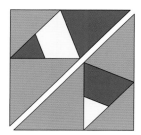

4 | Assemble the block as shown.

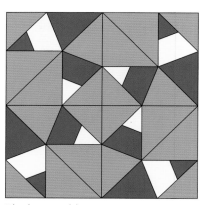

Block assembly

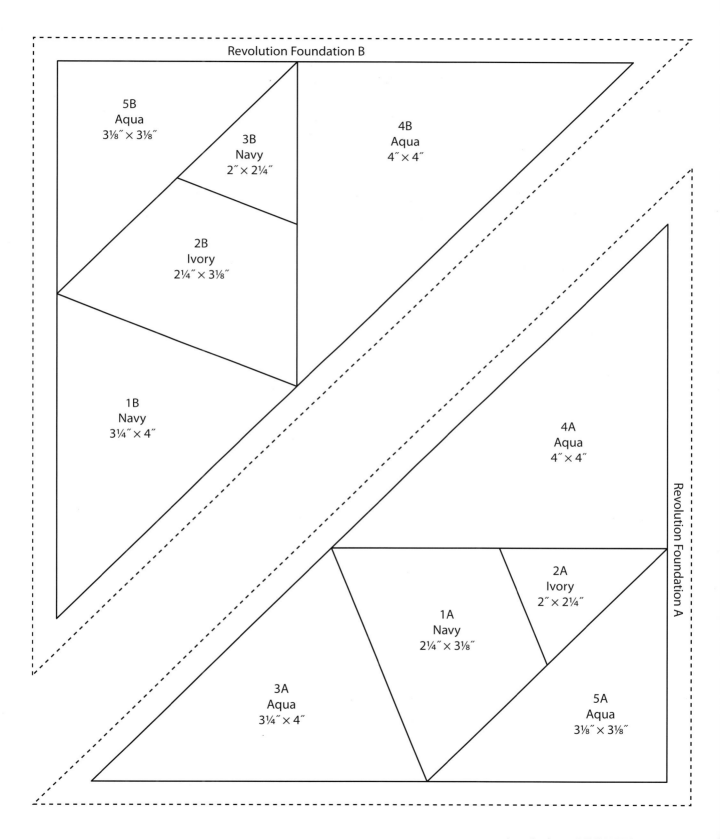

Revolution Foundation B

5B
Aqua
3⅛″ × 3⅛″

3B
Navy
2″ × 2¼″

4B
Aqua
4″ × 4″

2B
Ivory
2¼″ × 3⅛″

1B
Navy
3¼″ × 4″

4A
Aqua
4″ × 4″

2A
Ivory
2″ × 2¼″

1A
Navy
2¼″ × 3⅛″

3A
Aqua
3¼″ × 4″

5A
Aqua
3⅛″ × 3⅛″

Revolution Foundation A

Corsage

FINISHED BLOCK:
12″ × 12″

Block designed by Kerri Thomson with Dena Designs, sewn by Kerri Thomson

Fabric collection: FreeSpirit Marquesas by Dena Designs

Technique: Piecing

See this block in *Subdivision* (page 100).

Ingredients

BLACK PRINT: 1 fat eighth

CORAL PRINT: ¼ yard

WHITE PRINT: ⅛ yard

Cutting

BLACK PRINT
• Cut 4 squares 4½″ × 4½″.

CORAL PRINT
• Cut 1 square 4½″ × 4½″.
• Cut 16 squares 2½″ × 2½″.

WHITE PRINT
• Cut 8 squares 2½″ × 2½″.

Construction

Note: All seam allowances are a scant ¼″. See arrows on the illustrations for pressing direction.

1 │ Use 2 coral 2½″ squares to sew triangle corners (page 119) to the top of a black 4½″ square. Make 4.

2 │ Use the remaining coral and white 2½″ squares to make four-patch units. Make 4.

3 │ Assemble the block as shown.

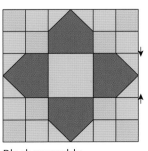

Block assembly

Arizona

FINISHED BLOCK:
12″ × 12″

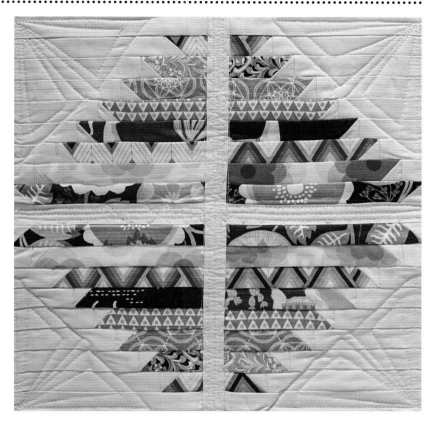

Block designed by Kerri Thomson with Joel Dewberry, sewn by Kerri Thomson

Fabric collection: FreeSpirit Florabelle by Joel Dewberry

Technique: Piecing

See this block in *Tribal* (page 104).

Ingredients

GRAY/GOLD PRINTS:
A variety to total ¼ yard

BLACK/ORANGE PRINTS:
A variety to total ¼ yard

NATURAL SOLID: ¼ yard

Cutting

Note: Label the pieces as they are cut.

GRAY/GOLD PRINTS
- Cut 2 rectangles 1⅛″ × 1¾″ (A).
- Cut 2 rectangles 1⅛″ × 2⅜″ (B).
- Cut 2 rectangles 1⅛″ × 3″ (C).
- Cut 2 rectangles 1⅛″ × 3⅝″ (D).
- Cut 2 rectangles 1⅛″ × 4¼″ (E).
- Cut 2 rectangles 1⅛″ × 4⅞″ (F).
- Cut 2 rectangles 1⅛″ × 5½″ (G).
- Cut 2 rectangles 1⅛″ × 6⅛″ (H).

BLACK/ORANGE PRINTS
Cut the same pieces as for the gray/gold prints.

NATURAL SOLID
- Cut 32 squares 1⅛″ × 1⅛″ for end squares.
- Cut 4 rectangles 1⅛″ × 6⅛″ for horizontal sashing.
- Cut 2 rectangles 1¼″ × 6⅛″ for center horizontal sashing.

- Cut 1 rectangle 1¼″ × 12½″ for vertical sashing.
- Cut 4 rectangles 1⅛″ × 4⅞″ (A).
- Cut 4 rectangles 1⅛″ × 4¼″ (B).
- Cut 4 rectangles 1⅛″ × 3⅝″ (C).
- Cut 4 rectangles 1⅛″ × 3″ (D).
- Cut 4 rectangles 1⅛″ × 2⅜″ (E).
- Cut 4 rectangles 1⅛″ × 1¾″ (F).
- Cut 4 squares 1⅛″ × 1⅛″ (G).

Construction

Note: All seam allowances are a scant ¼″. See arrows on the illustrations for pressing direction.

1 | Draw a line diagonally on the wrong side of the 32 end squares.

2 | Place an end square on one end of a gold rectangle A, right sides together, noting the direction of the drawn line. Sew on the line, trim the corner to ¼″ seam allowance (page 119). Repeat to make 2 of each gold rectangle.

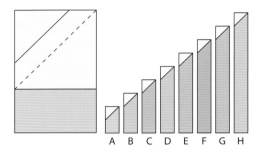

A B C D E F G H

3 | Repeat Step 2 to make 2 of each orange rectangle, reversing the direction of the drawn line. Make 2 of each rectangle.

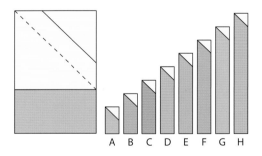

A B C D E F G H

4 | Sew an A background rectangle to the A gold rectangle. Repeat with the corresponding pieces for the remaining background rectangles. Make 2 of each.

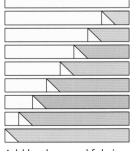

Add background fabric to gold strips.

5 | Assemble the gold/background rectangles into a corner unit. Make 2. Add a horizontal sashing strip to the top of each unit.

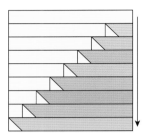

6 | Repeat Steps 4 and 5 using the orange rectangles.

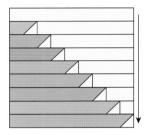

7 | Assemble the block as shown.

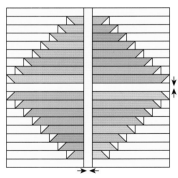

Block assembly

On Target

**FINISHED BLOCK:
12″ × 12″**

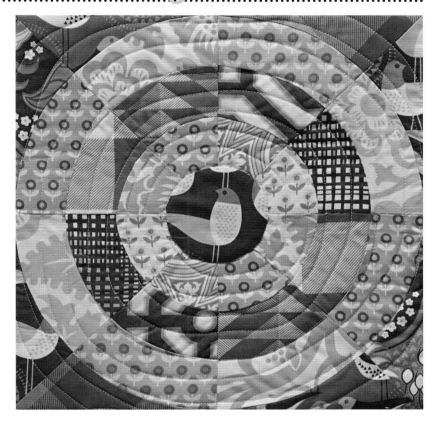

Block designed by Kerri Thomson with Joel Dewberry, sewn by Kerri Thomson

Fabric collection: FreeSpirit Modernist by Joel Dewberry

Techniques: Piecing, appliqué

See this block in *Subdivision* (page 100).

Ingredients

YELLOW PRINTS: ¼ yard total of 2 fabrics

GRAY PRINTS: ¼ yard total of 2 fabrics

GOLD PRINTS: ⅛ yard total of 2 fabrics

GREEN PRINTS: ⅛ yard total of 4 fabrics

TURQUOISE PRINTS: ⅛ yard total of 4 fabrics

TEMPLATE PLASTIC

ON TARGET PATTERNS (page 24 and 25):
Make 1 copy of each pattern.
(To download, see page 6.)

Cutting

Trace and cut the circle; curves 1, 2, and 3; and backgrounds 1 and 2 from template plastic. Trace the template on the right side of the fabric and cut on the drawn lines.

YELLOW PRINTS
• Cut 4 curve 1.
• Cut 4 curve 3.

GRAY PRINTS
• Cut 4 curve 3.

GOLD PRINTS
• Cut 4 curve 1.

GREEN PRINTS
• Cut 4 curve 2.
• Cut 2 background 1.
• Cut 2 background 2.

TURQUOISE PRINTS
• Cut 4 curve 2.
• Cut 2 background 1.
• Cut 2 background 2.
• Cut 1 circle for center.

Construction

Note: All seam allowances are a scant ¼˝. See arrows on the illustrations for pressing direction.

1 | Arrange the curves and background pieces to form a bull's-eye.

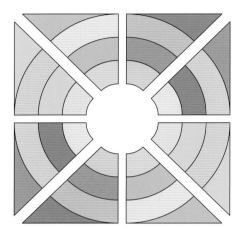

2 | Sew each curve 1, 2 and 3 and a background piece into a segment. Find the center of each curve and pin with the inside curve on top, then line up and pin the side edges. Sew along the pinned edge, gently pulling the edges to fit between the pins. Make 8 segments.

3 | Sew the segments together in pairs. Press the seams open. Make 4 quadrants.

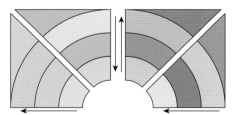

Sew curves into 8 segments. Sew pairs together.

4 | Sew the quadrants together. Press the seams open.

5 | Stabilize the center of the bull's-eye by pressing a freezer-paper square to the back of the center hole.

6 | Turn under the seam allowance on the center circle and press. Center the circle on the block, ensuring the pressed edge covers the seam allowance of the hole and press to the freezer paper. Appliqué by hand or machine along the folded edge. Remove the freezer paper.

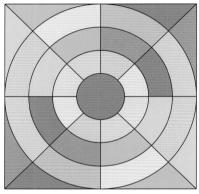

Block assembly

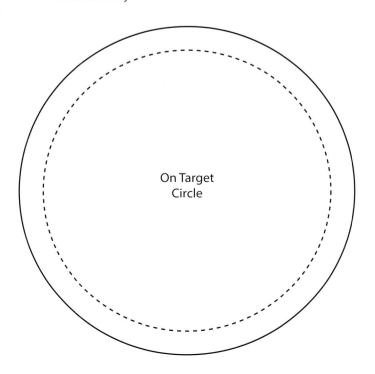

On Target
Circle

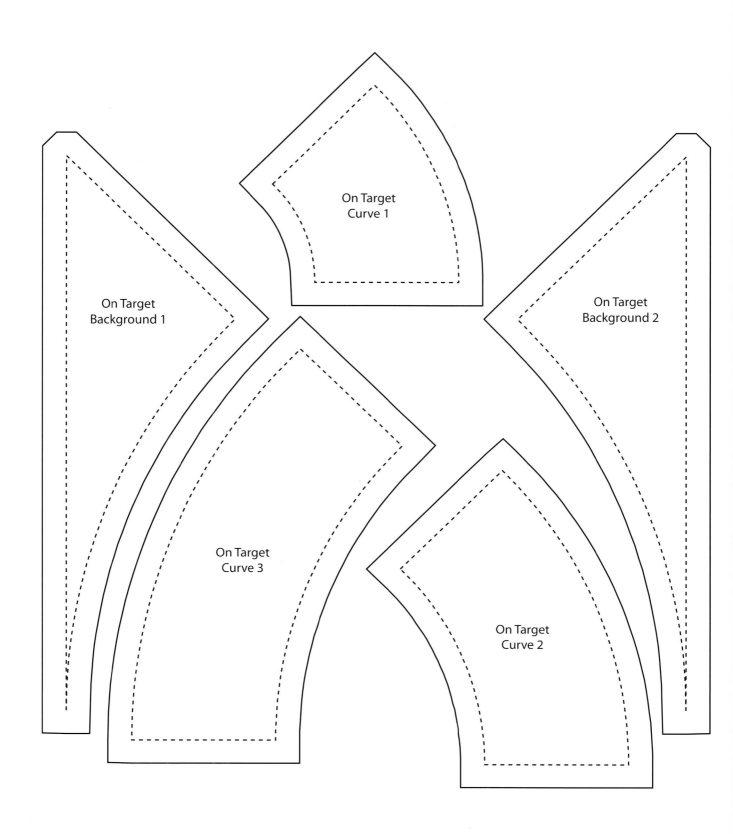

On Target
Curve 1

On Target
Background 1

On Target
Background 2

On Target
Curve 3

On Target
Curve 2

Sunset

FINISHED BLOCK:
12″ × 12″

Block designed by Kerri Thomson with Joel Dewberry, sewn by Kerri Thomson

Fabric collection: FreeSpirit Florabelle by Joel Dewberry

Technique: Piecing

See this block in *Tribal* (page 104).

Ingredients

GRAY/GOLD PRINTS:
A variety to total
¼ yard

BLACK/ORANGE
PRINTS: A variety
to total ⅛ yard

NATURAL SOLID:
¼ yard

Cutting

GRAY/GOLD PRINTS
- Cut 1 square 4½″ × 4½″.
- Cut 7 squares 2⅞″ × 2⅞″.

BLACK/ORANGE PRINTS
- Cut 7 squares 2⅞″ × 2⅞″.

NATURAL SOLID
- Cut 2 squares 4½″ × 4½″.
- Cut 14 squares 2⅞″ × 2⅞″.

Construction

Note: All seam allowances are a scant ¼″.
See arrows on the illustrations for pressing direction.

1 | Using the gray/gold and natural solid 2⅞″ squares, make 14 half-square triangles (page 119). Note: This includes extra half-square triangles to allow for a scrappier look.

2 | Sew 4 gray/gold half-square triangles together to form a four-patch unit. Make 3. You will have 2 extras.

3 | Repeat Steps 1 and 2 with the black/orange and natural solid 2⅞″ squares to make 3 black/orange four-patch units.

4 | Assemble the block as shown.

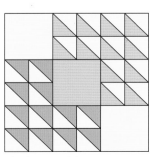

Block assembly

Star Popper

FINISHED BLOCK:
12″ × 12″

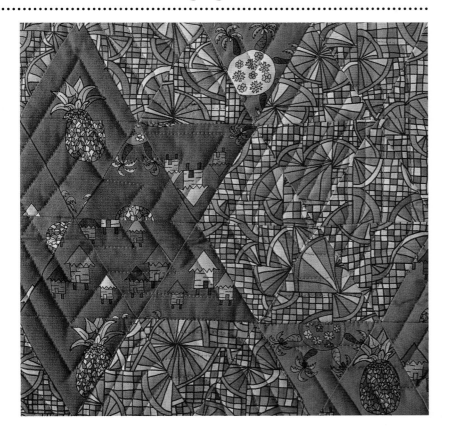

Block designed and sewn by
Kathy Doughty

Fabric collection: FreeSpirit Folk
Art Revolution and Celebrate by
Kathy Doughty

Technique: Piecing

See this block in *Neighbors* (page 114).

Ingredients

WAGON WHEELS PRINT:
4″ × width of fabric

PURPLE PRINT: 4″ × width of fabric

TEAL PRINT: 4″ × width of fabric

60° TRIANGLE RULER

Cutting

Use the 60° triangle ruler to cut the triangles.

WAGON WHEELS PRINT

• Cut 1 strip 3½″ × width of fabric.
  Subcut 13 full triangles, 2 half-triangles facing
  right, and 2 half-triangles facing left.

PURPLE PRINT

• Cut 1 strip 3½″ × width of fabric.
  Subcut 8 full triangles, 1 half-triangle facing left,
  and 1 half-triangle facing right.

TEAL PRINT

• Cut 1 strip 3½″ × width of fabric.
  Subcut 3 full triangles, 1 half-triangle facing left,
  and 1 half-triangle facing right.

Construction

*Note: All seam allowances
are a scant ¼″. Press the
seams open.*

Assemble the block as
shown. Match and pin the
seam intersections as you
sew the rows together.

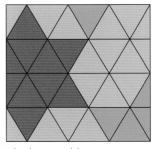

Block assembly

Value Matters

FINISHED BLOCK:
12″ × 12″

Block designed and sewn by Kathy Doughty

Fabric collection: FreeSpirit Flock Together, Folk Art Revolution, and Celebrate by Kathy Doughty

Techniques: Piecing, appliqué

See this block in *Subdivision* (page 100).

Ingredients

DARK-VALUE PRINT: ⅓ yard

MEDIUM-VALUE PRINT: ⅓ yard

LIGHT-VALUE PRINT: ⅓ yard

TEMPLATE PLASTIC

22½° WEDGE RULER: Or make a template from the Value Matters pattern (page 30). (To download, see page 6.)

Cutting

Use the wedge ruler or a template made from the pattern to cut the wedges.

ALL PRINTS

• Cut 1 strip 7¾″ × width of fabric from each.

From the dark and medium fabrics: Subcut 4 wedges each.

From the light print: Subcut 8 wedges.

DARK-VALUE PRINT

• Cut 1 circle 3½″ in diameter.

Construction

Note: All seam allowances are a scant ¼˝. Press the seams open.

1 | Arrange the wedges as shown.

2 | Sew the wedges together in pairs. Join the pairs.

3 | Continue to join the pairs and wedges until they form a circle.

4 | Trim the block to 12½˝ square. To make the cut, center the corners of a 12½˝ square ruler in the center of the medium wedges.

5 | Make a 3˝ circle template out of card stock. Use a running stitch to sew around the outer seam allowance of the fabric circle. Place the template in the middle of the circle and pull the threads to gather the fabric. Knot. Press the circle with an iron and carefully remove the template.

6 | Appliqué the circle to the center of the block.

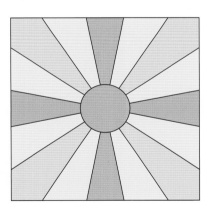

Block assembly

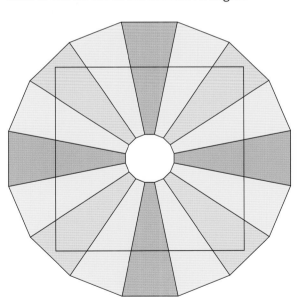

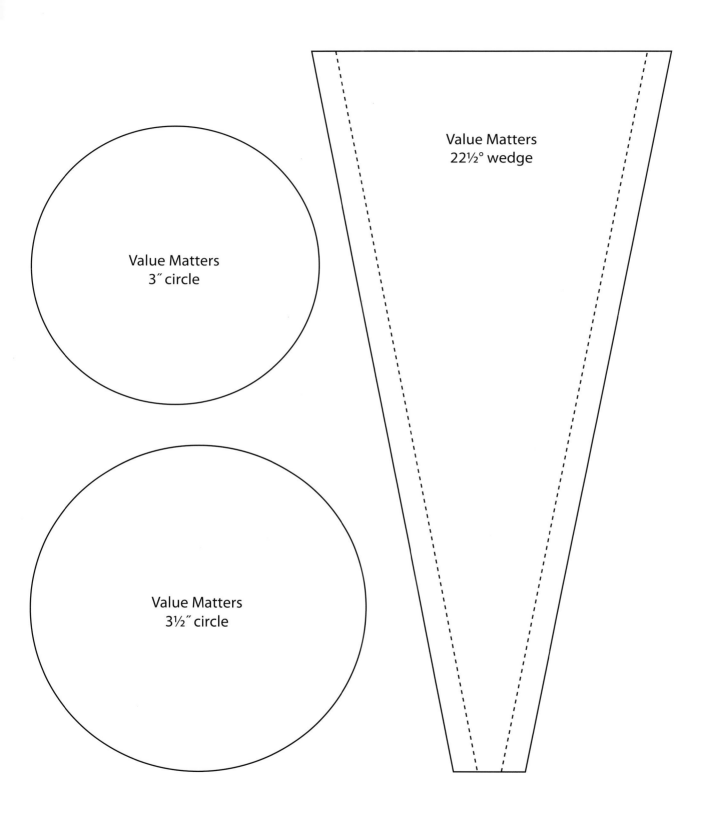

Value Matters
3″ circle

Value Matters
3½″ circle

Value Matters
22½° wedge

Spun

FINISHED BLOCK:
12″ × 12″

Block designed by Margot Elena, sewn by Kerri Thomson

Fabric collection: FreeSpirit Library of Flowers: Stories & Songbirds by Margot Elena

Technique: Piecing

See this block in *Neighbors* (page 114).

Ingredients

BLUE FLORAL PRINT: 1 fat eighth

PINK PRINT: 1 fat eighth

GREEN LARGE FLORAL PRINT: 1 fat eighth

GREEN SMALL FLORAL PRINT: 1 fat eighth

Cutting

BLUE FLORAL PRINT
• Cut 2 squares 4¾″ × 4¾″.

PINK PRINT
• Cut 2 squares 4¾″ × 4¾″.

GREEN LARGE FLORAL PRINT
• Cut 1 square 7¼″ × 7¼″.
  Subcut in half diagonally twice.

GREEN SMALL FLORAL PRINT
• Cut 1 square 7¼″ × 7¼″.
  Subcut in half diagonally twice.

Construction

Note: All seam allowances are a scant ¼″.
See arrows on the illustrations for pressing direction.

1 | Sew the center squares together to form a four-patch unit.

2 | Sew the triangles together in pairs. Make 4.

3 | Assemble the block as shown.

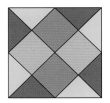

Block assembly

Collage Basket

FINISHED BLOCK: 12″ × 12″

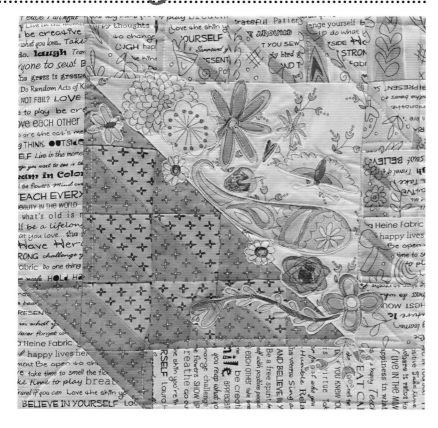

Block designed and sewn by Laura Heine

Fabric collection: FreeSpirit The Dress by Laura Heine

Techniques: Piecing, raw-edge fusible appliqué

See this block in *Cozy* (page 108).

Ingredients

PINK STRIPE, BLUE PRINT, AND GREEN PRINT: ⅛ yard of each

TEXT PRINT: ¼ yard
(or ⅓ yard if directional)

BLOSSOM PRINT: 1 square 10″ × 10″

GARDEN PRINT: 1 square 10″ × 10″

DOUBLE-SIDED FUSIBLE WEB:
½ yard (such as Steam-A-Seam 2, by The Warm Company)

Cutting

PINK STRIPE PRINT
- Cut 4 squares 2⅞″ × 2⅞″.
  Subcut in half diagonally.
- Cut 1 square 2½″ × 2½″.

BLUE PRINT
- Cut 6 squares 2⅞″ × 2⅞″.
  Subcut in half diagonally.

GREEN PRINT
- Cut 3 squares 2⅞″ × 2⅞″.
  Subcut in half diagonally.

BLOSSOM PRINT
- Cut 1 square 8⅞″ × 8⅞″.
  Subcut in half diagonally.
  You will have 1 extra triangle.

TEXT PRINT
- Cut 4 squares 2⅞″ × 2⅞″.
  Subcut in half diagonally.
- Cut 2 rectangles 2½″ × 8½″.
- Cut 1 square 4⅞″ × 4⅞″.
  Subcut in half diagonally.
  You will have 1 extra triangle.

Construction

Note: All seam allowances are a scant ¼″. See arrows on the illustrations for pressing direction.

1 | Make 6 half-square triangles by sewing the blue and green triangles together.

2 | Arrange the half-square triangles and remaining blue triangles as shown and assemble into vertical rows. Sew the rows together to make the basket body.

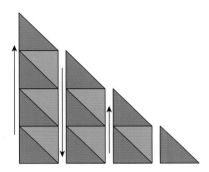

3 | Sew the large print triangle to the pieced basket.

4 | Make 8 half-square triangles by sewing the pink stripe and text print triangles together.

5 | Sew 2 sets of 4 half-square triangles and a pink stripe 2½″ square together as shown for the basket handles. Join each pieced unit to the basket.

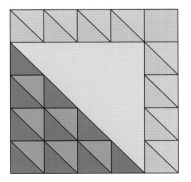

6 | Sew a blue triangle to the short end of each text print rectangle and join to the basket, referring to the block assembly diagram (below).

7 | Sew the remaining background triangle to the bottom of the basket. Press the seam toward the background.

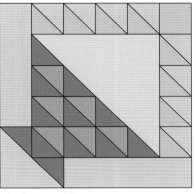

Block assembly

8 | Stick the double-sided fusible web onto the back of the 10″ green garden square. Cut out the motifs. Remove the backing paper from the cut motifs and arrange them in the basket. Once you have your basket arranged how you like it, fuse it in place following the manufacturer's directions.

Melon Flower

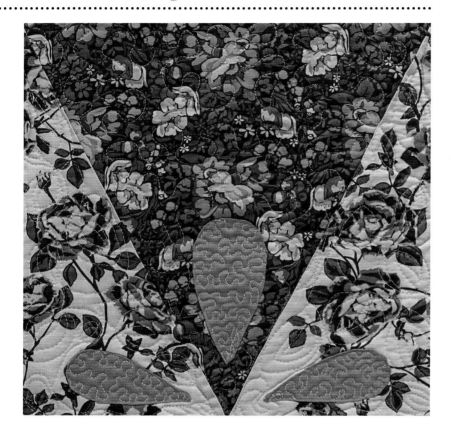

Block designed by Anna Maria Horner, sewn by Kerri Thomson

Fabric collection: FreeSpirit Floral Retrospective by Anna Maria Horner

Techniques: Piecing, appliqué (raw-edge fusible or needle-turn)

See this block in *Tribal* (page 104).

Ingredients

DARK FLORAL PRINT: 1 fat quarter

LIGHT FLORAL PRINT: 1 fat quarter

PINK SOLID: 1 square 10˝ × 10˝

FUSIBLE WEB: 1 square 10˝ × 10˝

TEMPLATE PLASTIC

MELON FLOWER SMALL AND LARGE PETAL PATTERNS (page 35): Make 1 copy of each pattern. (To download, see page 6.)

Cutting

PINK SOLID

• Cut 2 small petals and 1 large petal.

For hand appliqué: Trace the small and large appliqué petals onto template plastic and cut out. Trace around the template on the right side of the fabric and cut ¼˝ from the shapes to add a seam allowance.

For fusible machine appliqué: Trace the small and large appliqué petals onto the paper side of the fusible web and cut ¼˝ outside the drawn lines. Follow the manufacturer's instructions to fuse the drawn shapes to the wrong side of the fabrics and then cut along the drawn lines.

DARK FLORAL PRINT

• Cut 1 square 12¾˝ × 12¾˝.

LIGHT FLORAL PRINT

• Cut 1 rectangle 13¼˝ × 13¼˝, centering the rose print.

Construction

Note: All seam allowances are a scant ¼″. See arrows on the illustrations for pressing direction.

1 | Fold the 12¾″ dark floral square in half, wrong sides together, matching the side edges. With the folded edge on the right side, cut along the diagonal from the top left to bottom right. Open the fold and press the center triangle flat. Discard the smaller triangles.

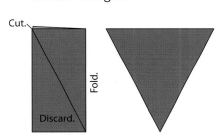

2 | Repeat Step 1 with the 13¼″ light floral square. This time, keep the 2 side triangles and discard the large triangle.

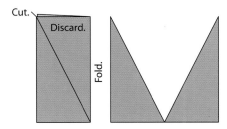

3 | Sew the center and side triangles together. Trim the block to 12½″ × 12½″.

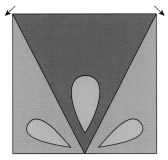

Block assembly

4 | Place the 2 small petals and large petal on top of the block and appliqué in place.

For hand appliqué: Machine baste the petals on the traced line. Hand stitch by removing 1″ of the basting stitches, folding the raw edge under along the perforated stitching line, and stitching in place. Repeat to stitch completely around the shapes.

For machine appliqué: Fuse the petals in place and use a zigzag or blind stitch to appliqué around the edge.

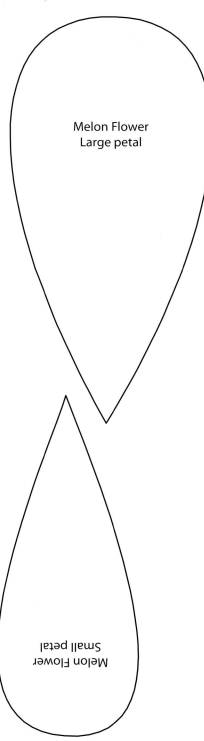

Melon Flower
Large petal

Melon Flower
Small petal

Kaleidoscope

**FINISHED BLOCK:
12″ × 12″**

Block designed by Kaffe Fassett with Liza Prior Lucy, sewn by Liza Prior Lucy

Fabric collection: Kaffe Fassett Classics and fabric designed by Kaffe Fassett, Brandon Mably, and Philip Jacobs as part of the Kaffe Fassett Collective for FreeSpirit

Technique: Piecing

See all 3 colorways of this block in *Over Here* (page 96).

Ingredients

LARGE- OR MEDIUM-SCALE PRINT: ¼ yard or more with 8 identical motifs. To determine the exact yardage, locate 8 motifs on the fabric.

SMALL PRINT OR SOLID: 1 rectangle 5″ × 10″

TEMPLATE PLASTIC

PENCIL

KALEIDOSCOPE BLADE PATTERN (next page): Make 1 copy of the pattern. (To download, see page 6.)

Cutting

TEMPLATE PLASTIC

• Trace the kaleidoscope blade pattern (next page) onto the plastic and cut out the template. Locate the motif you wish to cut and place the template on that motif. With the pencil, trace some of the details. This will help you line up the template to cut each motif identically.

LARGE- OR MEDIUM-SCALE PRINT

• Fussy cut 8 identical patches using the template.

SMALL PRINT

• Cut 2 squares 4½″ × 4½″. Subcut in half diagonally.

Construction

Note: All seam allowances are a scant ¼″. Press the seams open.

1 | Sew the blades together along the long edges.

2 | Sew the small print or solid triangles to the corners as shown. Trim the block to 12½″ × 12½″.

Alternate colorways of Kaleidoscope

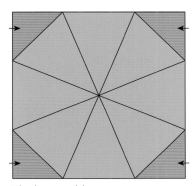

Block assembly

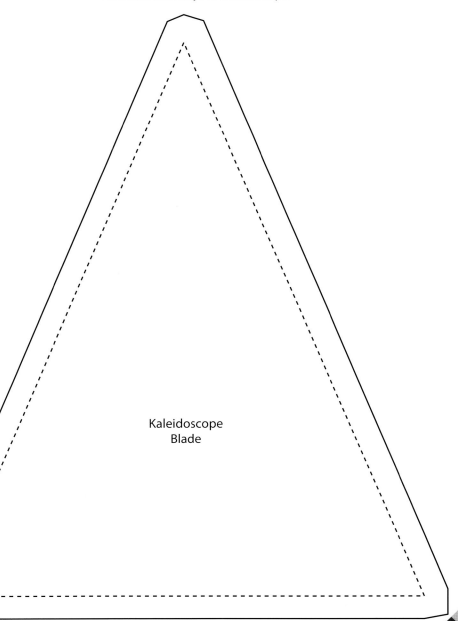

Kaleidoscope
Blade

Askew

FINISHED BLOCK: 12″ × 12″

Block designed by Erin McMorris, sewn by Kerri Thomson

Fabric collection: FreeSpirit Intermix by Erin McMorris

Technique: Foundation paper piecing

See this block in *Neighbors* (page 114).

Ingredients

BLACK PRINT: 1 square 5″ × 5″

GREEN PRINTS: 6 prints to total ½ yard

CREAM PRINT: 1 fat eighth

ASKEW FOUNDATION PATTERN (next page): Make 1 copy of the pattern at 200%, or download the pattern in quadrants, print full-size, and tape them together. (To download, see page 6.)

Cutting

BLACK PRINT
• Cut 1 square 4½″ × 4½″.

GREEN PRINTS (TOTAL OF 6)
• Cut 12 rectangles 3″ × 14″ from assorted prints.

CREAM PRINT
• Cut 3 rectangles 3″ × 14″.

Construction

Press each seam as it is sewn, using a dry iron.

1 | Refer to Foundation Paper Piecing (page 120) to piece the block. Start by placing the center rectangle over the segment 1 paper foundation. Randomly choosing prints, add rectangles to the center following the numerical order on the paper foundation.

2 | Trim the block to 12½″ × 12½″. Remove the papers in reverse order.

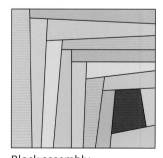

Block assembly

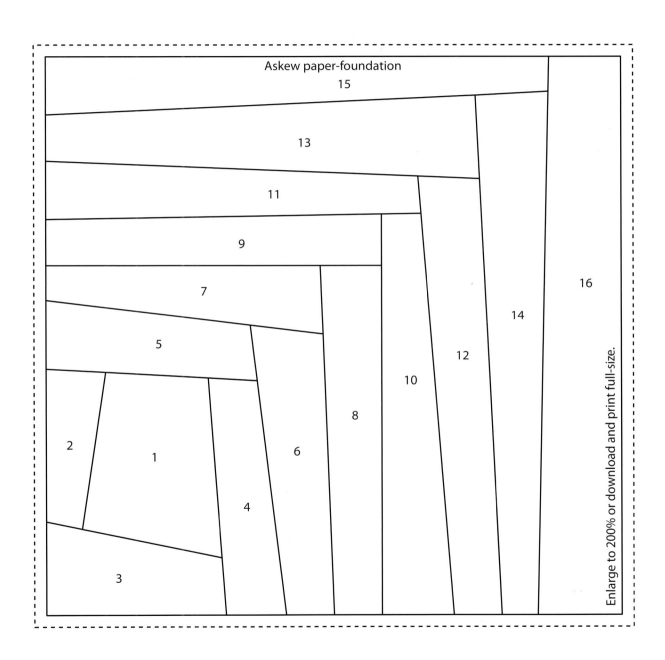

Askew paper-foundation

15

13

11

9

7

5

16

14

12

10

8

6

2

1

4

3

Enlarge to 200% or download and print full-size.

Spooled

FINISHED BLOCK: 12″ × 12″

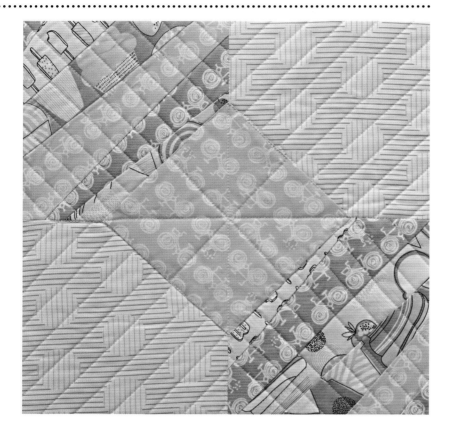

Block designed by Erin McMorris, sewn by Kerri Thomson

Fabric collection: FreeSpirit Sugar by Erin McMorris

Techniques: Piecing, string piecing to fabric foundation

See this block in *Subdivision* (page 100).

Ingredients

ORANGE BICYCLE PRINT: 1 fat eighth

PINK AND ORANGE PRINTS: A variety to total ¼ yard

LOW-VOLUME PRINT: 1 fat eighth

MUSLIN: 1 fat eighth

Cutting

ORANGE BICYCLE PRINT

- Cut 1 square 5½″ × 5½″.

- Cut 2 angled strips 10″ long, varying width at each end between 1″ and 3″.

PINK AND ORANGE PRINTS

- Cut 16 angled strips 10″ long, varying width at each end between 1″ and 2½″.

LOW-VOLUME PRINT

- Cut 2 squares 6½″ × 6½″ for corner squares.

MUSLIN

- Cut 2 squares 7″ × 7″ for foundations.

Construction

Note: All seam allowances are a scant ¼″. Press each seam as it is sewn.

1 Randomly select 2 strips and place right sides together, aligning a long edge. Place this pair on top of a muslin foundation square, slightly off a diagonal. Sew through all 3 layers. Press and open the top strip.

 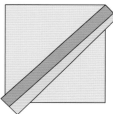

2 | Repeat the process with a third strip. Continue adding strips until you have covered the entire foundation square.

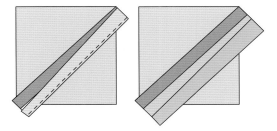

3 | Turn the foundation square right side down and trim to 6½″ × 6½″. Make 2.

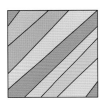

4 | Place a corner square on a cutting mat. Measure and mark 2⅞″ down the right edge and across the bottom edge. Draw a line connecting the marks. Cut on this line. Make 2 corners.

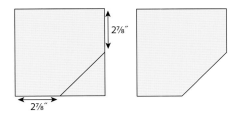

5 | Repeat Step 4 with the foundation squares. Note the direction of the seams when marking. Make 2.

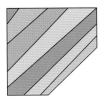

6 | Pin the diagonal edge of a corner square to an edge of the 5½″ center square, right sides together. Stitch along the pinned edge, starting and stopping ¼″ from the side edges. Press the seam towards the center square.

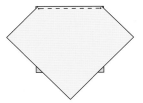

7 | Repeat Step 6 to add the second corner to the opposite side of the center square and the foundation squares to the remaining sides.

8 | Pin the center square in half diagonally, right sides together, matching the corner edges. Starting at the outside edge, sew along the pinned edge, stopping at the seam with the center square. Press the seam open. Repeat to sew the remaining corner edges together.

 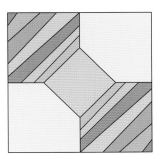

Block assembly

Orange Peel

FINISHED BLOCK:
12″ × 12″

Block designed and sewn by
Verna Mosquera

Fabric collections: FreeSpirit Love
& Friendship, Peppermint Rose,
and Fruta y Flor by Verna Mosquera

Techniques: Piecing, appliqué

See this block in *Subdivision*
(page 100).

Ingredients

WHITE WITH RED DOT: 1 fat eighth

WHITE WITH RED HEARTS:
1 square 6″ × 6″

GREEN PLAID: 1 fat eighth

PINK STRIPE: 1 square 6″ × 6″

GREEN AND PINK FLORAL:
1 square 6″ × 6″

GREEN TONE-ON-TONE: 1 fat
eighth for petals

PINK POLKA DOT:
1 fat eighth for petals

GREEN/PINK GEOMETRIC:
1 fat eighth for petals

PINK FLORAL PRINT:
1 fat eighth for petals

LIGHT PINK SOLID: 1 fat eighth

LIGHT GREEN SOLID: 1 fat eighth

FREEZER PAPER

**APPLIQUÉ NEEDLE, THREAD,
AND PINS**

EMBROIDERY NEEDLE

EMBROIDERY FLOSS: 4 shades of
pink and 2 shades of green

SEWLINE MARKING PENCIL

TEMPLATE PLASTIC

**ORANGE PEEL PETAL PATTERN
(page 44):** Make 1 copy of the
pattern. (To download, see
page 6.) Make a petal template.

Cutting

WHITE WITH RED DOT

• Cut 1 square 4¾″ × 4¾″.

• Cut 2 squares 4″ × 4″.
Subcut in half diagonally.
You will have 1 extra triangle.

WHITE WITH RED HEARTS

• Cut 1 square 4″ × 4″.
Subcut in half diagonally.

GREEN PLAID

• Cut 4 squares 4″ × 4″.
Subcut in half diagonally.
You will have 1 extra triangle.

PINK STRIPE

• Cut 1 square 4¾″ × 4¾″.

GREEN AND PINK FLORAL

• Cut 1 square 4¾″ × 4¾″.

SOLID PINK

• Cut 2 squares 4″ × 4″.
Subcut in half diagonally.
You will have 1 extra triangle.

• Cut 1 square 3½″ × 3½″.

SOLID GREEN

• Cut 2 squares 4″ × 4″.
Subcut in half diagonally.
You will have 1 extra triangle.

GREEN TONE-ON-TONE,

PINK POLKA DOT,

GREEN/PINK GEOMETRIC,

AND PINK FLORAL PRINTS

• Use the petal template to
make 4 petals from each
fabric. See Appliqué and
Embroidery (at right).

Construction

Block Assembly

Note: All seam allowances are a scant ¼″.
See arrows on the illustrations for pressing directions.

1 │ For Unit 1, join a triangle (3 white with red dot, 1 white with red hearts) to each side of the pink stripe square.

2 │ For Unit 2, center and sew a triangle (4 green plaid) to each side of the green and pink floral square.

3 │ For Unit 3, make a half-square triangle by joining a pink solid triangle to a green plaid triangle. Make 3.

4 │ For Unit 4, center and sew a triangle (3 green solid, 1 white with red hearts) to each side of the white-with-red-dot square.

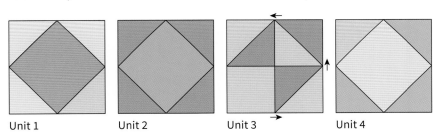

Unit 1   Unit 2   Unit 3   Unit 4

5 │ Square up the 4 units to 6½″ × 6½″ each. Piece together the top and bottom rows, pressing the seams in opposite directions. Join the rows into a four-patch unit.

Appliqué and Embroidery

1 │ Trace the petal shape onto the matte side of the freezer paper. Cut on the line with paper scissors. Press the shiny side down onto right side of appliqué fabric.

2 │ Trace a turning line using the Sewline marking pencil right along the cut edge of the freezer-paper template shape.

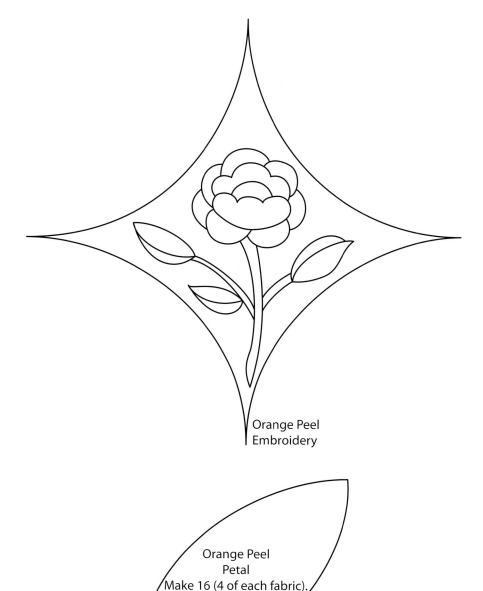

Orange Peel
Embroidery

Orange Peel
Petal
Make 16 (4 of each fabric).

3 | Leaving the freezer paper on the fabric, cut around the petal shape, leaving approximately ⅛″ all the way around the shape. Prepare 4 leaves from each of 4 different fabrics for a total of 16 petals.

4 | Appliqué each petal using your favorite appliqué method.

5 | Place the block over a light box and use the Sewline marking pencil to trace the rose embroidery pattern (at left) onto the blank area in the center of Unit 4. Using the stem stitch and 2 strands of floss, embroider the rose using 4 different shades of pink and 2 shades of green. Press the block from the wrong side.

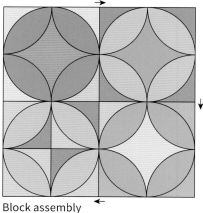

Block assembly

Snowy Owl

FINISHED BLOCK:
12″ × 12″

Block designed and sewn by Verna Mosquera

Fabric collections: FreeSpirit Love & Friendship, Peppermint Rose, and Fruta y Flor by Verna Mosquera

Techniques: Piecing, appliqué

See this block in *Subdivision* (page 100).

Ingredients

WHITE WITH RED DOT: 1 fat eighth

GREEN PLAID: 1 fat eighth

MEDIUM PINK: 1 fat eighth

YELLOW FLORAL: 1 square 6″ × 6″

DARK PINK: 1 fat eighth

LIGHT PINK: 1 fat eighth

LIGHT PINK APPLIQUÉ THREAD

APPLIQUÉ NEEDLE

TEMPLATE PLASTIC

SEWLINE MARKING PENCIL

GLUE PEN

1″ HEXAGON PAPER PIECES: 7

Cutting

WHITE WITH RED DOT

• Cut 1 square 6⅛″ × 6⅛″.

• Cut 2 squares 4⅛″ × 4⅛″.
  Subcut in half diagonally twice.

GREEN PLAID

• Cut 2 squares 4⅛″ × 4⅛″.
  Subcut in half diagonally twice.

MEDIUM PINK

• Cut 2 squares 4⅛″ × 4⅛″.
  Subcut in half diagonally twice.

• Cut 4 squares 2½″ × 2½″.

YELLOW FLORAL

• Cut 1 square 5¼″ × 5¼″.
  Subcut in half diagonally twice.

DARK PINK

• Cut 2 squares 4⅞″ × 4⅞″.
  Subcut in half diagonally once.

• Cut 1 hexagon using the
  hexagon instructions (at right)
  and the pattern (next page).

LIGHT PINK

• Cut 6 hexagons using the
  hexagon instructions (at right)
  and the pattern (next page).

Construction

Note: All seam allowances are a scant ¼″.

See arrows on the illustrations for pressing direction.

Hexagons

1 | Trace around the edge of a 1″ hexagon paper piece onto a piece of clear template plastic. Add ⅜″ seam allowance around the drawn hexagon. Cut out the hexagon template with a rotary cutter and ruler.

2 | On the back of the dark pink fabric, center the hexagon template over a cluster of flowers. Trace around the template with a Sewline marking pencil. Cut on the marked line with scissors and set aside.

3 | Use the same method to fussy cut 6 hexagons around the heart motifs on the light pink fabric. To ensure identical placement of the image, trace the heart motif onto the center of the hexagon plastic template.

4 | Place a paper hexagon on the back side of a fabric hexagon. Using a glue pen, apply a dab of glue to one edge of the paper template. Fold the fabric over the edge and finger press. Work clockwise around the shape, gluing one side at a time until all fabric edges are turned. Make 7.

5 | Using a whipstitch, attach a heart hexagon to each side of the center flower hexagon. Once all 6 heart hexagons have been attached, remove the paper template from the center flower hexagon.

6 | Stitch the remaining seams between each heart hexagon. Press. Carefully remove the remaining paper templates and set aside.

Block Assembly

1 | Sew a white triangle to a medium pink triangle.

2 | Sew a white triangle and a green triangle to each side of medium pink square.

3 | Sew a medium pink triangle to a green triangle.

4 | Join together the units from Steps 1–3.

5 | Repeat Steps 1–4 to make 4 units.

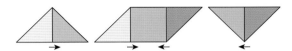

6 | Sew a dark pink triangle to the unit from Step 5. Make 4.

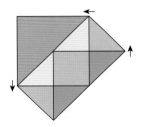

7 | Sew a yellow triangle to the ends of 2 of the units from Step 6.

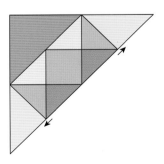

8 | Assemble the block as shown.

9 | Hand appliqué the hexagon flower to the center of the block. Press the block from the wrong side.

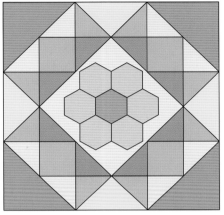

Block assembly

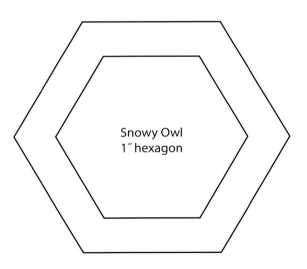

Snowy Owl
1″ hexagon

Agape

FINISHED BLOCK:
12″ × 12″

Block designed by Shannon Newlin, sewn by Kerri Thomson

Fabric collection: FreeSpirit Floral Waterfall by Shannon Newlin

Technique: Appliqué

See this block rotated 90° in *Tribal* (page 104).

Ingredients

GOLD FLORAL PRINT: 1 square 14″ × 14″ for background

BERRY PRINT: 1 fat eighth for appliqué

COLORFUL PRINT: 1 fat eighth for appliqué

TURQUOISE WAVE PRINT: 1 square 10″ × 10″ for appliqué

ORANGE SOLID: 1 square 5″ × 5″ for appliqué

BLACK SOLID: 1 fat eighth for appliqué

DOT PRINT: 1 square 10″ × 10″ for appliqué

FREEZER PAPER

AGAPE PATTERNS (pages 50 and 51): Make 1 copy of the semicircle, triangle, arrow, large circle, and small circle patterns. (To download, see page 6.)

Cutting

Trace 2 semicircles and 1 triangle, arrow, large circle, and small circle (pages 50 and 51) onto the matte side of freezer paper and cut on the drawn lines. Press the freezer-paper shapes to the wrong side of the fabrics and cut ¼″ from the shapes to add a seam allowance.

GOLD FLORAL PRINT

• Cut 1 square 12½″ × 12½″ for background.

BERRY PRINT

• Cut 1 semicircle.

COLORFUL PRINT

• Cut 1 semicircle.

TURQUOISE WAVE PRINT

• Cut 1 large circle.

ORANGE SOLID

• Cut 1 small circle.

BLACK SOLID

• Cut 1 arrow.

DOT PRINT

• Cut 1 triangle.

Construction

Note: All seam allowances are a scant ¼″.

1 | Sew the 2 semicircles together along the straight edges. Press the seams open.

2 | Sew a running stitch within the outer seam allowance of the pieced circle appliqué. Press the seam allowance to the wrong side, gently pulling the running stitch to gather excess fabric. Remove the freezer paper and center the circle on the background square, right sides up. Hand or machine appliqué around the folded edge.

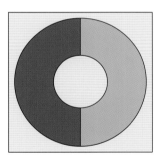

Appliqué pieced circle to background.

3 | Use the same method to prepare and appliqué the large circle over the center hole in the pieced circle.

4 | Prepare the arrow and triangle pieces, except do not press under the triangle edge that will be in the seam allowance of the block, nor the arrow inside, which will be tucked under the triangle. Position the arrow point at the center of the block, then place the triangle to cover the raw edge of the arrow, with the bottom raw edge of triangle aligned with the edge of the block. Appliqué in place.

5 | Prepare the small circle and appliqué in place.

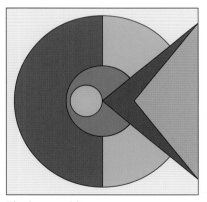

Block assembly

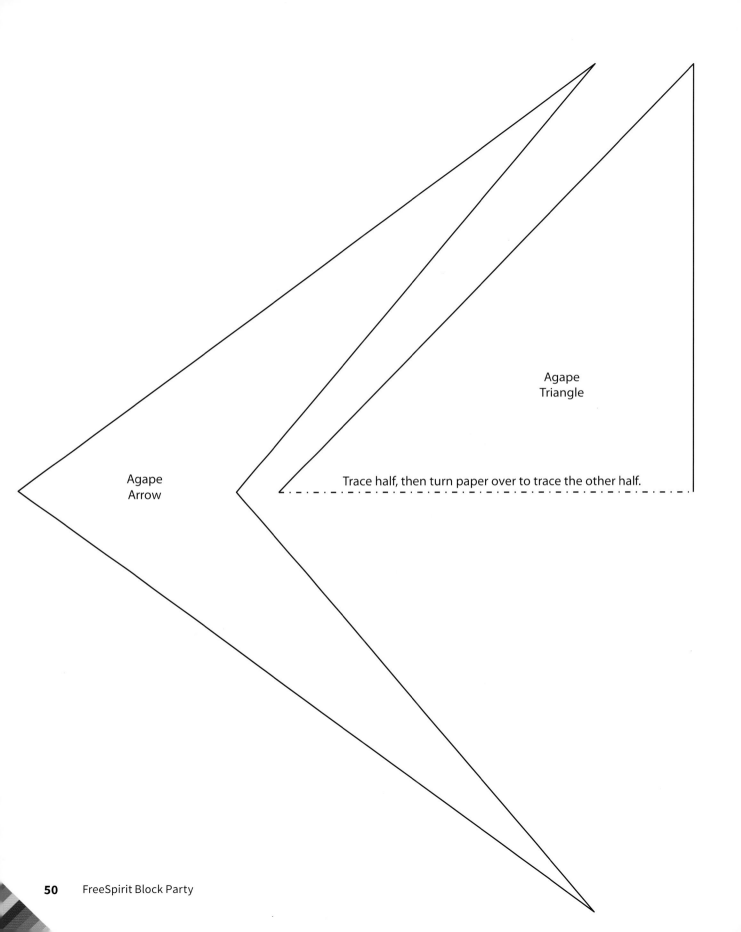

Agape
Triangle

Agape
Arrow

Trace half, then turn paper over to trace the other half.

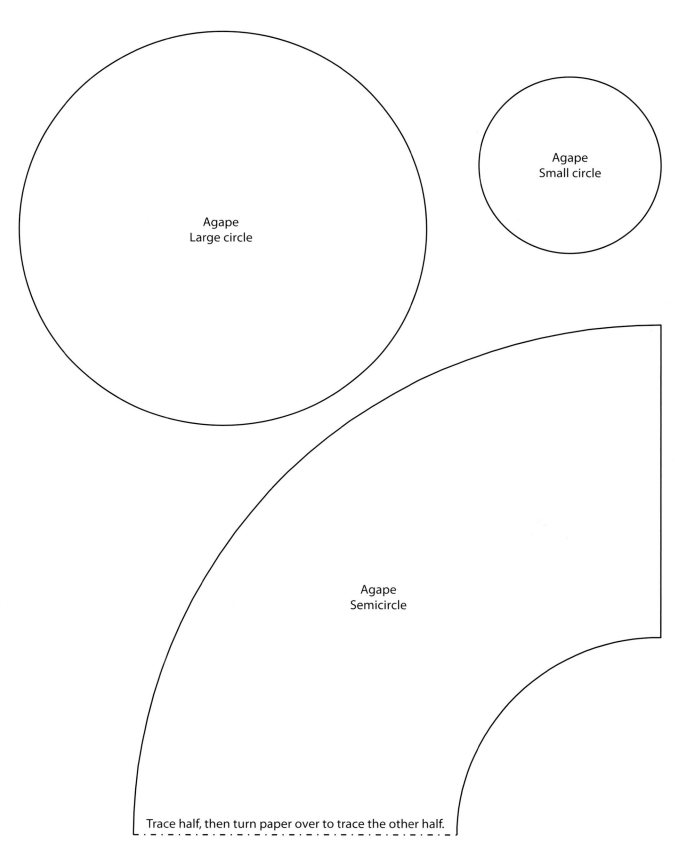

Agape
Large circle

Agape
Small circle

Agape
Semicircle

Trace half, then turn paper over to trace the other half.

London

FINISHED BLOCK:
12″ × 12″

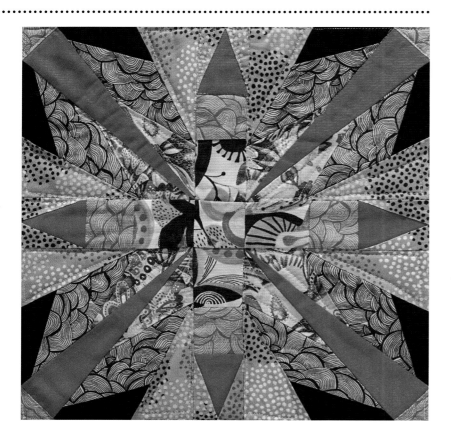

Block designed by Shannon Newlin, sewn by Kerri Thomson

Fabric collection: FreeSpirit Floral Waterfall by Shannon Newlin

Technique: Foundation paper piecing

See this block in *Tribal* (page 104).

Ingredients

LARGE FLORAL PRINT: 1 rectangle 3½″ × 16″

PINK WAVE PRINT: ⅛ yard

COLORFUL PRINT: ¼ yard

BLUE WAVE PRINT: ¼ yard

ORANGE SOLID: 1 fat eighth

BLACK SOLID: ⅛ yard

YELLOW DOT PRINT: ¼ yard

LONDON FOUNDATION PATTERNS A, B, AND C (page 54): Make 4 copies of each pattern. (To download, see page 6.)

Cutting

LARGE FLORAL PRINT

- Cut 1 square 2″ × 2″ for the center square.
- Cut 4 squares 3″ × 3″ (A1).

PINK WAVE PRINT

- Cut 4 squares 2½″ × 2½″ (A2).
- Cut 4 rectangles 2″ × 3″ (B6).

COLORFUL PRINT

- Cut 8 rectangles 2½″ × 6½″ (B4 and C4).

BLUE WAVE PRINT

- Cut 8 rectangles 3¼″ × 6″ (B2 and C2).

ORANGE SOLID

- Cut 4 squares 3″ × 3″ (A3).
- Cut 4 rectangles 3″ × 8″ (B5).

BLACK SOLID

- Cut 8 rectangles 2″ × 4″ (B1 and C1).

YELLOW DOT PRINT

- Cut 8 rectangles 2″ × 3¼″ (A4 and A5).
- Cut 8 rectangles 4″ × 6½″ (B3 and C3).

Construction

Note: All seam allowances are a scant ¼″.
Press each seam as it is sewn, using a dry iron.

1 │ Refer to Foundation Paper Piecing (page 120) to piece the A, B, and C foundations in order, matching the fabric to the sections listed on the paper. Make 4 of each.

2 │ Trim the foundations triangles on the outside solid line. Do not remove the paper yet.

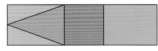

Unit A

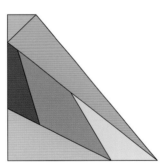

Unit B

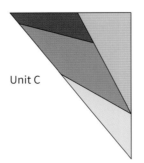

Unit C

3 │ Sew the B and C units together to make corner squares. Remove the papers from the seam allowances and press open. Make 4.

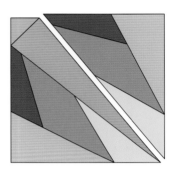

4 │ Assemble the block as shown.

Block assembly

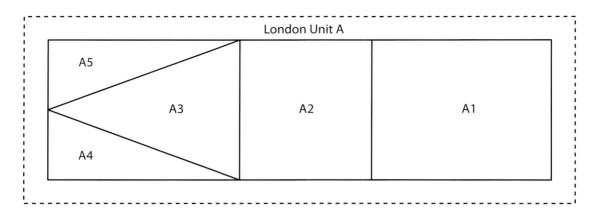

London Unit A

A5
A3
A4
A2
A1

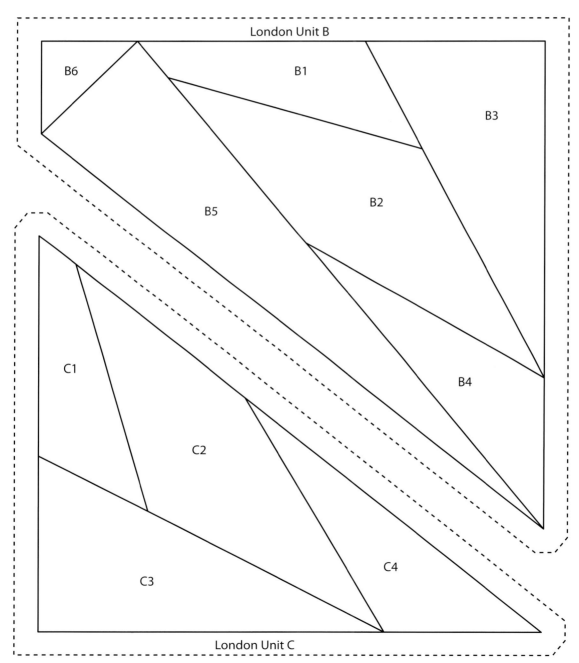

London Unit B

B6
B1
B3
B5
B2
B4

C1
C2
C3
C4

London Unit C

Judith's Fan

FINISHED BLOCK: 12″ × 12″

Block designed by Marsha Evans Moore with Jennifer Paganelli, sewn by Marsha Evans Moore

Fabric collection: FreeSpirit Judith's Fancy by Jennifer Paganelli

Technique: Foundation paper piecing

See this block in *Over Here* (page 96).

Ingredients

LARGE PRINTS: ¼ yard total of 5 different prints

MEDIUM OR SMALL PRINTS: ¼ yard total of 7 different prints

TEMPLATE PLASTIC

JUDITH'S FAN PATTERNS (pages 56–58): Make 2 copies of 3A and 1 copy each of 2B and 3B. (To download, see page 6.) Make plastic templates from the remaining patterns.

Cutting

Transfer the markings on the patterns for matching curved edges to the wrong side of the fabric.

LARGE PRINTS

• Cut 2 each 1A, 1B, 5A, and 5B, varying the fabrics as shown.

• Cut 1 each 2B and 3B.

MEDIUM AND SMALL PRINTS

• Cut 2 each from 2A, 4A, and 4B, varying the fabrics as shown.

Construction

Note: All seam allowances are a scant ¼″.
Press each seam as it is sewn, using a dry iron.

1 | Refer to Foundation Paper Piecing (page 120) to piece the 3A, 2B, and 3B foundations in order. Make 2 of 3A and 1 each of 2B and 3B.

2 | Trim the foundation pieces on the outside solid line. Remove the papers in reverse order.

3 | Arrange the pieces for 2 of quadrant A and 2 of quadrant B (note that quadrant B has 2 variations).

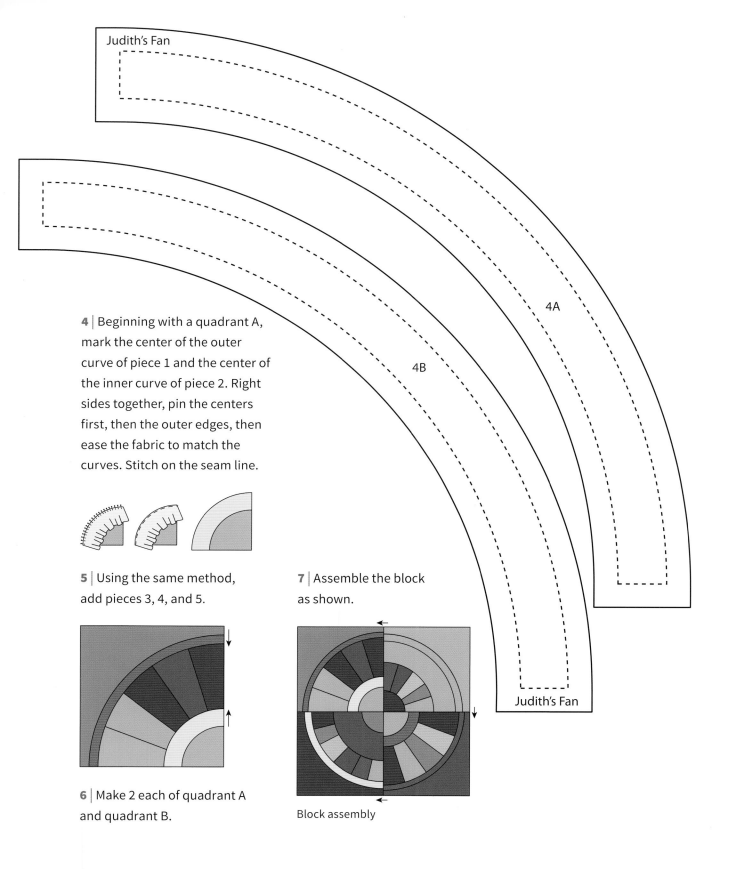

Judith's Fan

4A

4B

Judith's Fan

4 | Beginning with a quadrant A, mark the center of the outer curve of piece 1 and the center of the inner curve of piece 2. Right sides together, pin the centers first, then the outer edges, then ease the fabric to match the curves. Stitch on the seam line.

5 | Using the same method, add pieces 3, 4, and 5.

6 | Make 2 each of quadrant A and quadrant B.

7 | Assemble the block as shown.

Block assembly

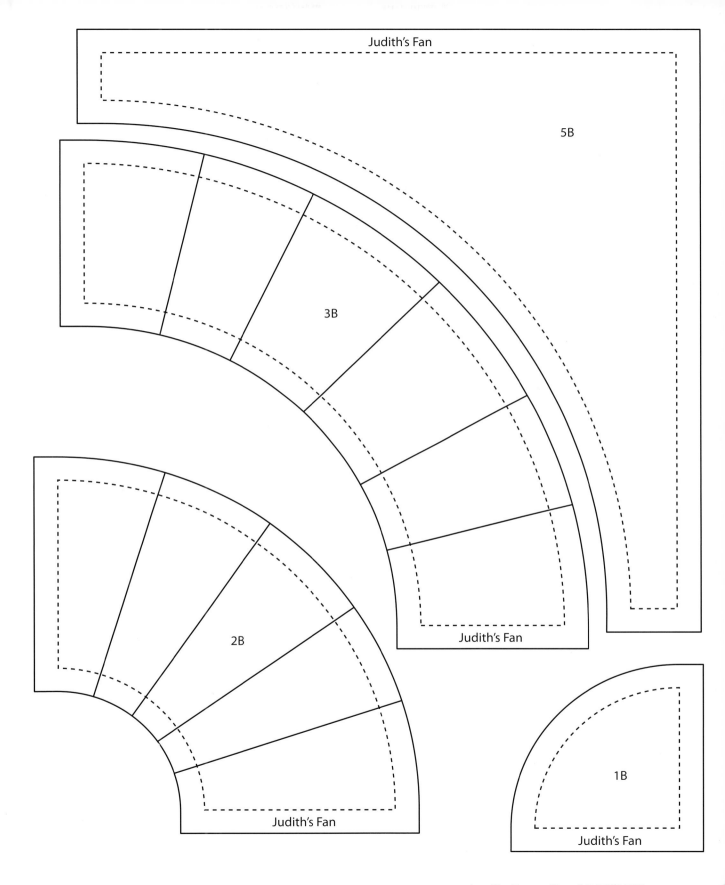

Judith's Fan

5B

3B

Judith's Fan

2B

Judith's Fan

1B

Judith's Fan

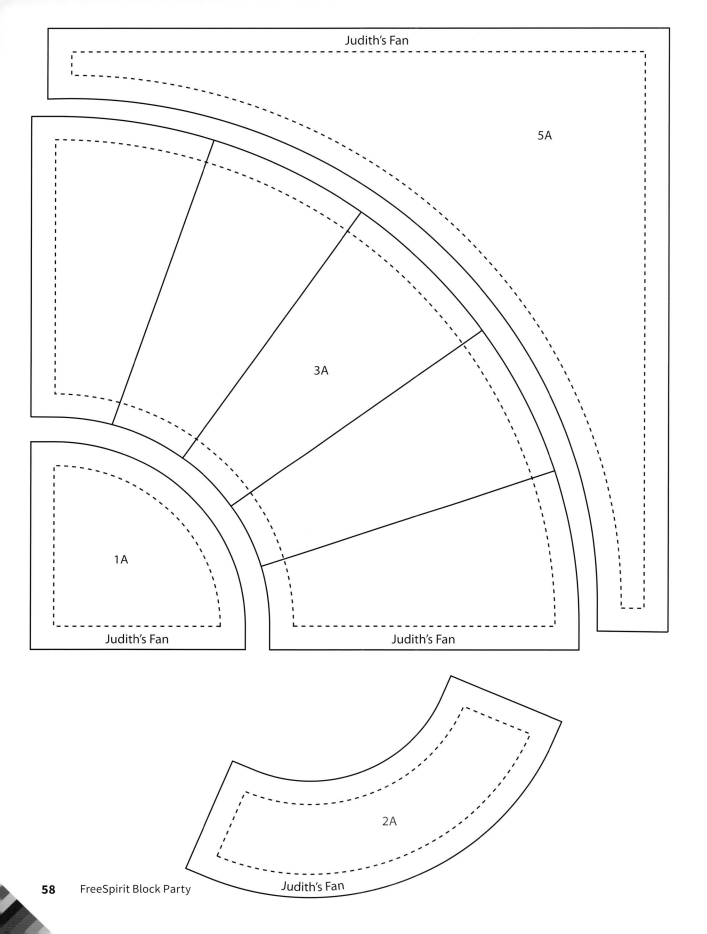

Judith's Fan

5A

3A

1A

Judith's Fan

Judith's Fan

2A

Judith's Fan

Sunny Isle Butterflies

FINISHED BLOCK:
12″ × 12″

Block designed by Marsha Evans Moore with Jennifer Paganelli, sewn by Marsha Evans Moore

Fabric collection: FreeSpirit Sunny Isle by Jennifer Paganelli

Technique: Piecing

See this block in *Subdivision* (page 100).

Ingredients

LARGE PRINTS (GREEN, BLUE, AND YELLOW):
⅛ yard total or scraps of 4 large prints

MONOCHROMATIC PRINTS (BLUE AND PINK):
Scraps of 3 prints

SMALL PRINTS (BLUE, GREEN, AND PINK): 3 scraps

PINK AND BLUE EMBROIDERY FLOSS

TEMPLATE PLASTIC

SUNNY ISLE BUTTERFLY PATTERNS (page 61):
Make 4 copies of each pattern or 1 copy on template plastic. (To download, see page 6.)

Cutting

Cut enough pieces for 4 butterflies. You may wish to make templates from plastic or tracing paper rather than regular paper if you wish to fussy cut the wing pieces.

LARGE PRINTS

• Cut 2 fore wings and 2 hind wings from each fabric, reversing the patterns for the second pieces. You may wish to fussy cut these pieces so the fabric design on the wings is somewhat symmetrical.

MONOCHROMATIC PRINTS

Fold each print in half, and use the templates to cut 2 shapes at the same time.

• From each of 2 prints, you will need 2 large triangles, 2 medium triangles, and 4 small triangles. From the third print, you will need 4 large and 4 medium triangles and 8 small triangles.

• For each butterfly, cut 1 body rectangle, 1 top rectangle, and 1 bottom rectangle from a single layer of fabric. Cut 1 set from each print, and choose 1 print to repeat. Make sure the body rectangles will contrast nicely with the wings and the other backgrounds.

SMALL PRINTS

• For each butterfly, cut 4 border triangles. Cut 2 sets with the template right side up for the upper left and lower right butterflies, and 2 reversed for the upper right and lower left butterflies. Cut 1 set from each print, and choose 1 print to repeat.

Construction

Note: All seam allowances are a scant ¼˝.
See arrows on the illustrations for pressing direction.

1 | Arrange the wings, background pieces, body, and border triangles for each butterfly.

2 | Sew a large triangle and a small triangle to each fore wing. Sew a medium triangle and small triangle to each hind wing.

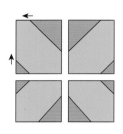

3 | Sew the fore wing units to the hind wing units.

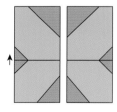

4 | Sew the background rectangles to the ends of the body.

5 | Sew the sides of the butterfly to the rectangle units.

6 | Sew a border triangle to each side of the butterfly.

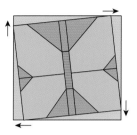

7 | Assemble the block as shown.

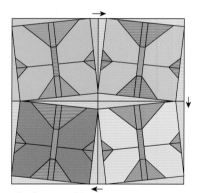

Block assembly

8 | Trace the pattern for the antennae to the top of each butterfly's body. Embroider the antennae with 2 strands of embroidery floss that matches the body, using small backstitches.

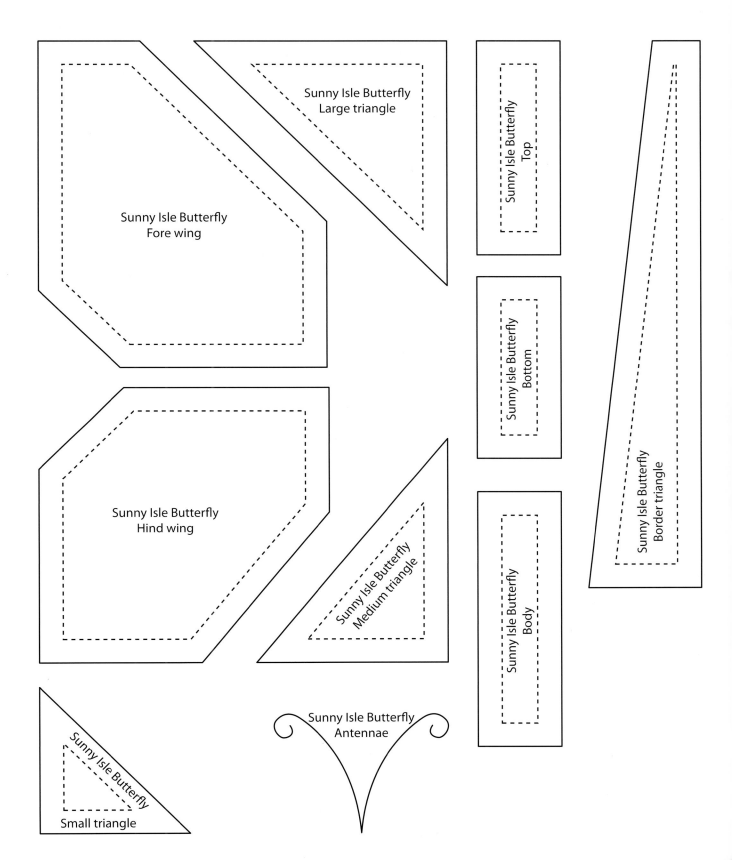

Sunny Isle Butterfly
Large triangle

Sunny Isle Butterfly
Fore wing

Sunny Isle Butterfly
Top

Sunny Isle Butterfly
Bottom

Sunny Isle Butterfly
Hind wing

Sunny Isle Butterfly
Medium triangle

Sunny Isle Butterfly
Border triangle

Sunny Isle Butterfly
Body

Sunny Isle Butterfly
Small triangle

Sunny Isle Butterfly
Antennae

Fly Away

FINISHED BLOCK: 12″ × 12″

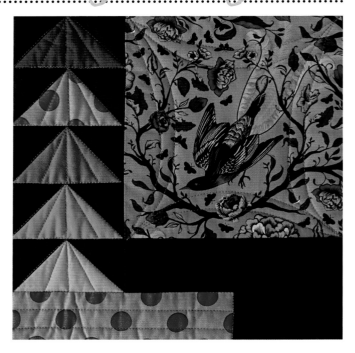

Block designed by Tula Pink with Kerri Thomson, sewn by Lindsay Conner

Fabric collection: FreeSpirit All Stars by Tula Pink

Technique: Piecing

See this block in *Neighbors* (page 114).

Ingredients

BLUE TAIL FEATHERS PRINT: 1 fat quarter

BLUE/RED DOT: 1 rectangle 3½″ × 15″

GREEN SOLID: 1 rectangle 3½″ × 15″

ROYAL SOLID: 1 rectangle 3½″ × 5½″

NAVY SOLID: ⅛ yard

Cutting

BLUE TAIL FEATHERS PRINT
- Cut 1 square 8½″ × 8½″, centering a bird design.

BLUE/RED DOT
- Cut 1 rectangle 2½″ × 8½″.
- Cut 1 rectangle 2½″ × 4½″.

GREEN SOLID
- Cut 3 rectangles 2½″ × 4½″.

ROYAL SOLID
- Cut 1 rectangle 2½″ × 4½″.

NAVY SOLID
- Cut 1 rectangle 2½″ × 8½″.
- Cut 1 rectangle 2½″ × 4½″.
- Cut 10 squares 2½″ × 2½″.

Construction

Note: All seam allowances are a scant ¼″.
See arrows on the illustrations for pressing direction.

1 | Using the navy solid 2½″ squares and 5 contrasting 2½″ × 4½″ rectangles, make 5 Flying Geese units (page 120).

2 | Sew the navy 2½″ × 8½″ rectangle to the bottom of the feature square.

3 | Sew the Flying Geese into a column, and join it to the left side of the feature square.

4 | Sew the remaining blue/red dot rectangle and navy rectangle together and add to the bottom of the block.

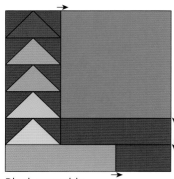

Block assembly

Tidepool

FINISHED BLOCK: 12″ × 12″

Block designed by Tula Pink with Kerri Thomson, sewn by Lindsay Conner

Fabric collection: FreeSpirit All Stars by Tula Pink

Technique: Piecing

See this block in *Neighbors* (page 114).

Ingredients

GREEN PRINT: 1 fat eighth

RED SOLID: 1 rectangle 2½″ × 16″

GREEN SOLID: 1 rectangle 2½″ × 3½″

GREEN DOT: ¼ yard

Cutting

GREEN PRINT
• Cut 1 square 7½″ × 7½″, centering a print design.

RED SOLID
• Cut 1 rectangle 1½″ × 8½″.
• Cut 1 rectangle 1½″ × 5½″.

GREEN SOLID
• Cut 1 rectangle 1½″ × 2½″.

GREEN DOT
• Cut 2 rectangles 2½″ × 12½″.
• Cut 2 rectangles 2½″ × 8½″.

Construction

Note: All seam allowances are a scant ¼″.
See arrows on the illustrations for pressing direction.

1 | Sew the green solid rectangle to the smaller red rectangle.

2 | Sew the pieced unit to the bottom of the center square; join the remaining red rectangle to the right edge.

3 | Assemble the block as shown.

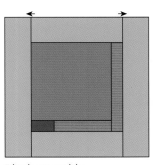

Block assembly

Wildwood

Block designed by Tula Pink with Kerri Thomson, sewn by Lindsay Conner

Fabric collection: FreeSpirit All Stars by Tula Pink

Technique: Piecing

See this block in *Neighbors* (page 114).

Ingredients

PURPLE OWL PRINT: 1 fat quarter

PURPLE BEE PRINT: 1 fat eighth

GREEN SOLID: 1 rectangle 3½″ × 9½″

AQUA/PURPLE DOT: 1 fat eighth

Cutting

PURPLE OWL PRINT
- Cut 1 rectangle 6½″ × 10½″, centering an owl design.
- Cut 1 square 2½″ × 2½″.

PURPLE BEE PRINT
- Cut 1 square 4½″ × 4½″, centering a bee design.

GREEN SOLID
- Cut 1 rectangle 2½″ × 8½″.

AQUA/PURPLE DOT
- Cut 1 rectangle 2½″ × 8½″.
- Cut 1 rectangle 4½″ × 8½″.

Construction

Note: All seam allowances are a scant ¼″.
See arrows on the illustrations for pressing direction.

1 | Sew the small print square to the top of the green solid rectangle and join the unit to the left edge of the large purple owl print rectangle.

2 | Sew the aqua/purple dot 2½″ rectangle to the top of the unit from Step 1.

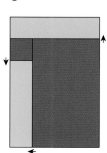

3 | Sew the bee square to the top of the aqua/purple dot 4½″ rectangle and join the unit to the left edge of the block.

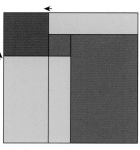

Block assembly

Mod Cabin

FINISHED BLOCK: 12″ × 12″

Block designed by Amy Reber, sewn by Kerri Thomson

Fabric collection: FreeSpirit Posy by Amy Reber

Technique: Foundation paper piecing

See this block in *Neighbors* (page 114).

Ingredients

PURPLE PRINT: 1 rectangle 4″ × 12″

GREEN PRINT: ⅛ yard

BLUE PRINT: ⅛ yard

PINK PRINT: ⅛ yard

FLORAL PRINT: ¼ yard

GREEN-BLUE PRINT: ¼ yard

MOD CABIN LEFT FOUNDATION AND RIGHT FOUNDATION PATTERNS (pages 66 and 67): Make 2 copies of each pattern. (To download, see page 6.)

Cutting

PURPLE PRINT
- Cut 4 rectangles 2¼″ × 3¼″ (R1, L1).

GREEN PRINT
- Cut 8 rectangles 1½″ × 3¼″ (R2, R3, L2, L3).

BLUE PRINT
- Cut 8 rectangles 1¾″ × 4″ (R4, R5, L4, L5).

PINK PRINT
- Cut 8 rectangles 1½″ × 5″ (R6, R7, L6, L7).

FLORAL PRINT
- Cut 8 rectangles 2½″ × 6″ (R8, R9, L8, L9).

GREEN-BLUE PRINT
- Cut 8 rectangles 2½″ × 7″ (R10, R11, L10, L11).

Construction

Note: All seam allowances are a scant ¼″.
Press each seam as it is sewn, using a dry iron.

1 | Refer to Foundation Paper Piecing (page 120) to piece the left and right foundations in order. Make 2 of each.

2 | Trim the inside edges on the outside solid line.

Right foundation

Left foundation

3 | Assemble the block as shown. Trim to 12½″ × 12½″. Remove the papers in reverse order.

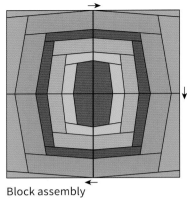

Block assembly

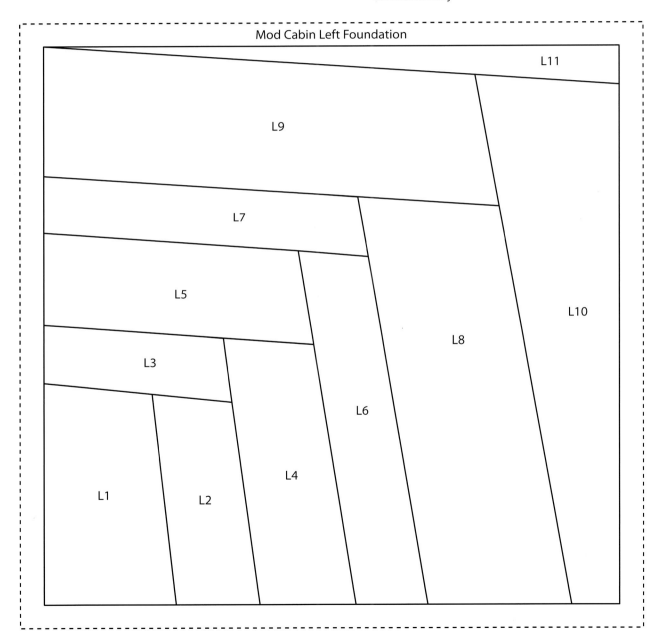

Mod Cabin Left Foundation

L11

L9

L7

L5

L3

L10

L8

L6

L1

L2

L4

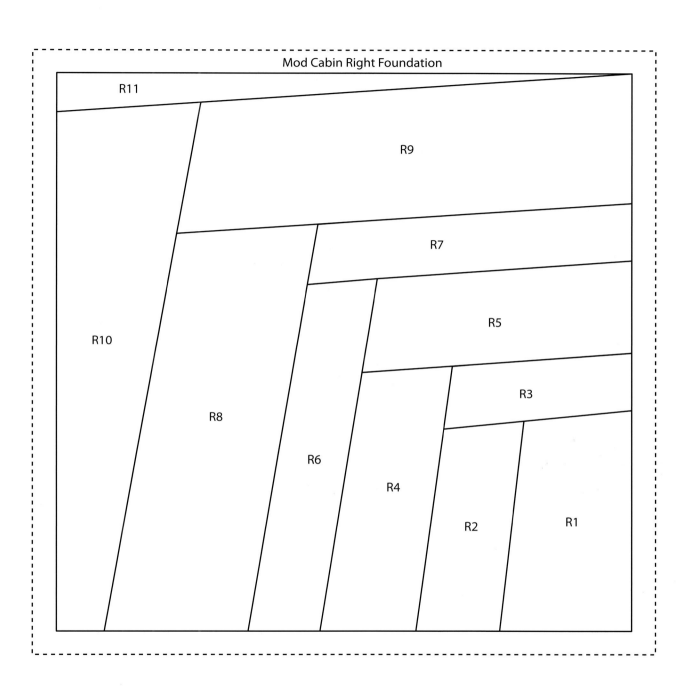

Mod Cabin Right Foundation

R11

R9

R7

R5

R10

R8

R6

R4

R3

R2

R1

Spinwheel

FINISHED BLOCK: 12″ × 12″

Block designed by Amy Reber, sewn by Kerri Thomson

Fabric collection: FreeSpirit Jitterbug by Amy Reber

Technique: Raw-edge fusible appliqué

See this block in *Subdivision* (page 100).

Ingredients

LIGHT BLUE PRINT: 1 fat quarter for background

DARK BLUE PRINT: 1 fat eighth for appliqué

GREEN PRINT: 1 fat quarter for appliqué

YELLOW PRINT: 1 square 10″ × 10″ for appliqué

FUSIBLE WEB: ¾ yard for appliqué

SPINWHEEL APPLIQUÉ MAP (next page): Make 1 copy of the pattern. (To download, see page 6.)

Cutting

Using the Spinwheel appliqué map (next page), trace 4 each of appliqué shapes 1, 2, and 3 onto the paper side of the fusible web and cut ¼″ outside the drawn lines. Follow the manufacturer's instructions to fuse the drawn shapes to the wrong side of the fabrics and then cut on the drawn lines.

LIGHT BLUE PRINT
• Cut 4 squares 6½″ × 6½″ for background.

DARK BLUE PRINT
• Cut 4 of shape 1.

GREEN PRINT
• Cut 4 of shape 2.

YELLOW PRINT
• Cut 4 of shape 3.

Construction

1 | Using the appliqué map as a guide, position one of each appliqué shape on top of a background square, right sides up. Remove the fusible web paper backing and fuse the appliqué shapes in place.

Using invisible thread, zigzag stitch the edges of the appliqué shape to secure. Make 4.

2 | Assemble the block as shown.

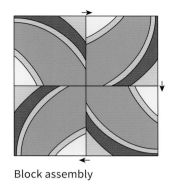

Block assembly

Spinwheel appliqué map

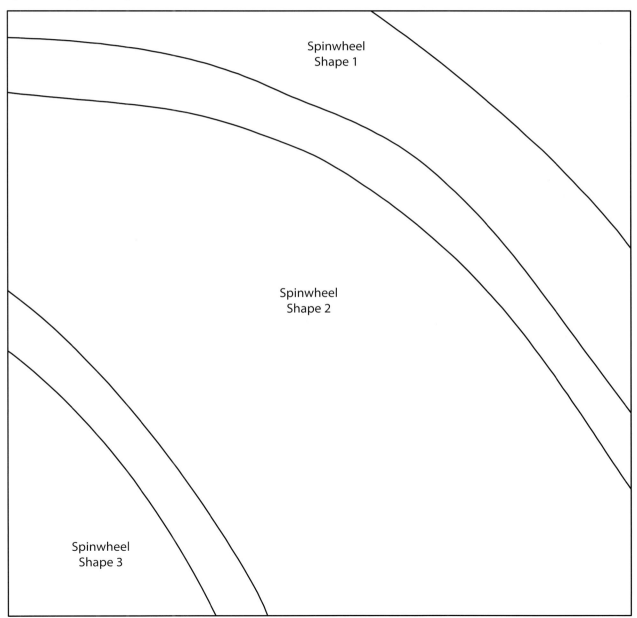

Spinwheel
Shape 1

Spinwheel
Shape 2

Spinwheel
Shape 3

Derailed

FINISHED BLOCK:
12″ × 12″

Block designed by Melissa Peda with Jane Sassaman, sewn by Melissa Peda

Fabric collection: FreeSpirit Spring Fever by Jane Sassaman and FreeSpirit Designer Essentials Solids

Technique: Piecing

See this block in *Tribal* (page 104).

Ingredients

BLACK PRINT: ⅛ yard

GREEN PRINT: ⅛ yard

WHITE SOLID: ⅛ yard

Cutting

BLACK PRINT, GREEN PRINT, AND WHITE
- Cut 1 strip 2½″ × width of fabric from each.

Construction

Note: All seam allowances are a scant ¼″. See arrows on the illustrations for pressing direction.

1 | Sew the strips together along the length with the black print fabric in the middle.

2 | Subcut 4 pieced squares 6½″ × 6½″ from the strip sets.

3 | Assemble the block as shown.

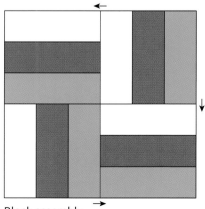

Block assembly

Maltese

FINISHED BLOCK:
12″ × 12″

Block designed by Melissa Peda with Jane Sassaman, sewn by Melissa Peda

Fabric collection: FreeSpirit Spring Fever by Jane Sassaman, FreeSpirit Scandia by Jane Sassaman, and FreeSpirit Designer Essentials Solids

Technique: Piecing

See this block in *Subdivision* (page 100).

Ingredients

RED PRINT: ¼ yard

STRIPED PRINT: ⅛ yard

WHITE SOLID: ⅛ yard

MALTESE KITE PATTERN (page 72):
Make 1 copy of the pattern.
(To download, see page 6.)

Cutting

Use the pattern (page 72) to make a plastic or paper template.

RED PRINT

• Cut 4 kite shapes. The pattern already includes the seam allowance.

STRIPED PRINT AND WHITE SOLID

• *From each:* Cut 1 strip 2½″ × width of fabric. Subcut into 2 equal lengths. You will have 1 leftover striped strip.

Construction

Note: All seam allowances are a scant ¼″.
See arrows on the illustrations for pressing direction.

1 Sew a striped strip between the 2 solid strips.

2 Cut 4 triangles from the strip set, using the 45° line on your ruler.

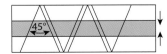

3 Assemble the block as shown.

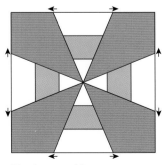

Block assembly

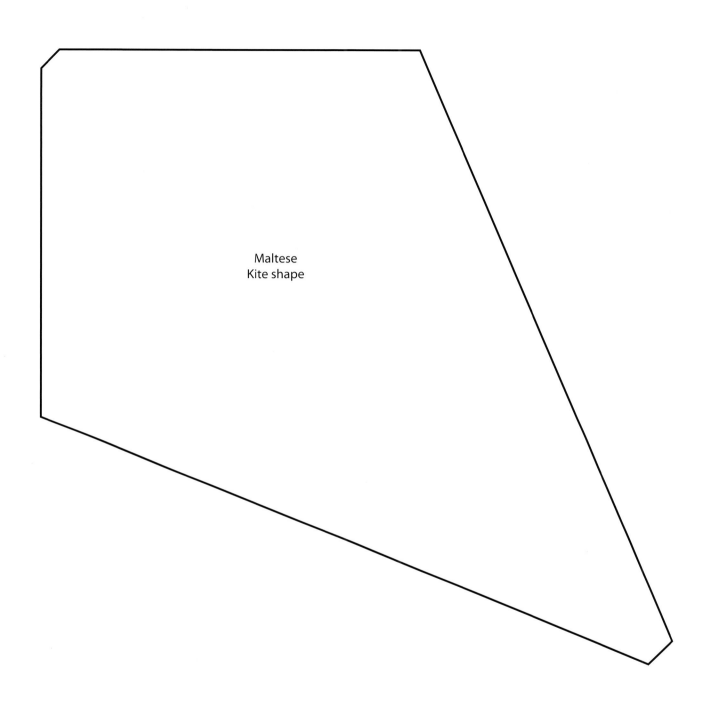

Maltese
Kite shape

Five Spot

FINISHED BLOCK: 12″ × 12″

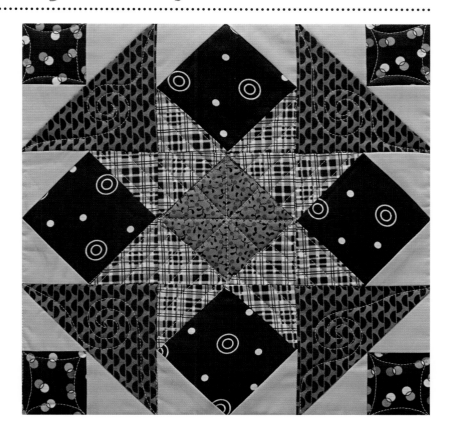

Block designed by Erica Jackman with Denyse Schmidt, sewn by Erica Jackman

Fabric collection: FreeSpirit Winter Walk by Denyse Schmidt, FreeSpirit Modern Solids selected by Denyse Schmidt

Technique: Foundation paper piecing

See this block in *Subdivision* (page 100).

Ingredients

BLUE PRINTS: 2 prints to total 1 fat eighth

BLACK PRINTS: 2 prints to total ⅛ yard

PLAID PRINT: ⅛ yard

GRAY SOLID: ⅛ yard

FIVE SPOT FOUNDATION PATTERNS (page 75): Make 5 copies of foundation A and 4 copies of foundation B. (To download, see page 6.)

Cutting

All pieces are cut generously to allow for wiggle room in foundation paper piecing.

BLUE PRINTS

• *From 1 print:* Cut 1 square 4″ × 4″ (A1).

• *From the second print:* Cut 2 squares 5½″ × 5½″. Subcut in half diagonally (B4).

BLACK PRINTS

• *From 1 print:* Cut 4 squares 4″ × 4″ (A1).

• *From the second print:* Cut 4 squares 3″ × 3″ (B1).

PLAID PRINT

• Cut 6 squares 3½″ × 3½″. Subcut in half diagonally (A2 and A3 on all A foundations and A4 and A5 on 1 foundation).

GRAY SOLID

• Cut 8 squares 3½″ × 3½″. Subcut in half diagonally (A4, A5, B2, and B3).

Construction

Note: All seam allowances are a scant ¼˝. Press each seam as it is sewn, using a dry iron.

1 | Refer to Foundation Paper Piecing (page 120) to piece the A and B foundations in order. Make 1 foundation A with a blue center square and all plaid corners; make the remaining 4 with a black center square and 2 plaid and 2 gray corners. Make 4 matching foundation B using the large blue triangles, black 3˝ squares, and gray triangles.

2 | Trim the foundation squares on the outside solid line. Remove the papers in reverse order.

3 | Assemble the block as shown.

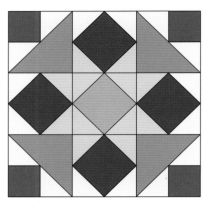

Block assembly

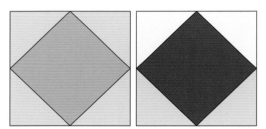

Foundation A units

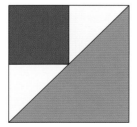

Foundation B units

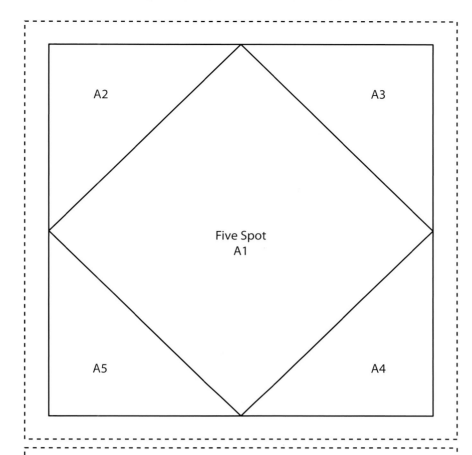

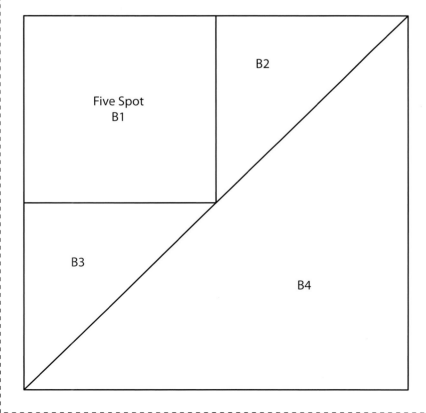

Denyse Schmidt

Snowbank

FINISHED BLOCK: 12″ × 12″

Block designed by Erica Jackman with Denyse Schmidt, sewn by Erica Jackman

Fabric collection: FreeSpirit Washington Depot by Denyse Schmidt

Technique: Piecing

See this block in *Subdivision* (page 100).

Ingredients

TEAL FLORAL: 1 fat eighth

LIME PRINT: ⅛ yard

PLAID PRINT: ¼ yard

Cutting

TEAL FLORAL
• Cut 4 squares 4½″ × 4½″.

LIME PRINT
• Cut 36 squares 1½″ × 1½″.

PLAID PRINT
• Cut 5 squares 4½″ × 4½″.

Construction

Note: All seam allowances are a scant ¼″. See arrows on the illustrations for pressing direction.

1 | Using the lime 1½″ squares, add a triangle corner (page 119) to all 4 corners of each teal and plaid 4½″ square.

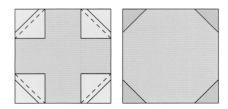

2 | Assemble the block as shown.

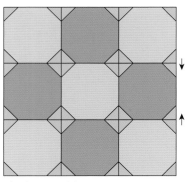

Block assembly

X Marks the Spot

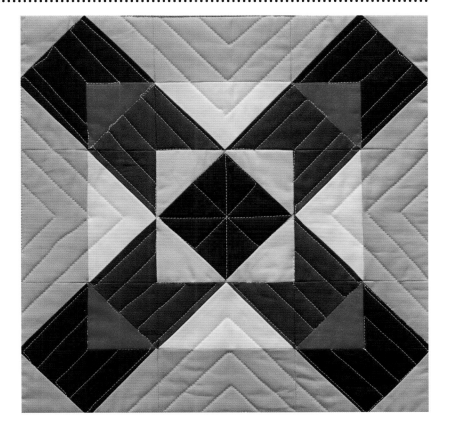

Block designed by Erica Jackman with Denyse Schmidt, sewn by Erica Jackman

Fabric collection: FreeSpirit Modern Solids selected by Denyse Schmidt

Technique: Piecing

See this block in *Subdivision* (page 100).

Ingredients

ROYAL BLUE (MINER BLUE): ⅛ yard

PURPLE-BLUE (FREEDOM BLUE): ⅛ yard

RED-ORANGE (SUNSET): ⅛ yard

TEAL (BALTIC BLUE): ⅛ yard

LIGHT BLUE (CARIBBEAN): ⅛ yard

WHITE (MIST): ⅛ yard

GRAY (SILVER): ⅛ yard

Cutting

ROYAL BLUE
• Cut 1 square 3¼″ × 3¼″.

PURPLE-BLUE
• Cut 6 squares 3″ × 3″.

RED-ORANGE
• Cut 2 squares 3″ × 3″.

TEAL
• Cut 2 squares 3″ × 3″.
• Cut 8 squares 2½″ × 2½″.

LIGHT BLUE
• Cut 2 squares 3″ × 3″.
  Subcut each in half diagonally.

WHITE
• Cut 4 rectangles 2½″ × 4½″.

GRAY
• Cut 4 rectangles 2″ × 4″.
• Cut 6 squares 3″ × 3″.

Construction

Note: All seam allowances are a scant ¼˝. See arrows on the illustrations for pressing direction.

1 | Sew a light blue triangle onto a side of the royal blue square. Press the seam open, then repeat with remaining triangles. Trim to 4½˝, making sure to leave an even seam allowance on each side of the square.

2 | Using the gray and purple-blue 3˝ squares, make 12 half-square triangles. Using the teal and red-orange 3˝ squares, make 4 half-square triangles (page 119). Trim to 2½˝ × 2½˝.

Make 12.   Make 4.

3 | Using the 2½˝ teal squares and the white rectangles, make 4 Flying Geese units (page 120).

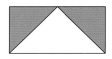

4 | Sew a gray 2½˝ × 4½˝ rectangle to each Flying Geese unit from Step 3 as shown.

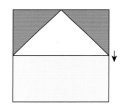

5 | Sew together 3 gray / purple-blue half-square triangles and 1 teal / red-orange half-square triangle to make a four-patch unit. Make 4.

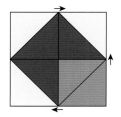

6 | Assemble the block as shown.

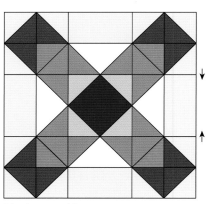

Block assembly

Four Points

FINISHED BLOCK:
12″ × 12″

Block designed by Linda and
Carl Sullivan with Snow Leopard
Designs, sewn by Lindsay Conner

Fabric collection: FreeSpirit Tribal
by Snow Leopard Designs, FreeSpirit
Designer Essentials Solids

Technique: Piecing

See this block in *Neighbors* (page 114).

Ingredients

PURPLE PRINT: 1/8 yard

BLACK TRIBAL PRINT: 1/8 yard

MEDIUM-SCALE TRIBAL PRINT:
1/8 yard

AQUA SOLID: 1 square 9″ × 9″

LARGE-SCALE TRIBAL PRINT:
1/8 yard

WHITE SOLID: 1 square 5″ × 5″

Cutting

PURPLE PRINT
- Cut 4 rectangles 2″ × 5″.
- Cut 4 rectangles 2″ × 3½″.

BLACK TRIBAL PRINT
- Cut 4 rectangles 2″ × 3½″.
- Cut 4 squares 2″ × 2″.

MEDIUM-SCALE TRIBAL PRINT
- Cut 8 rectangles 2″ × 3½″.

AQUA SOLID
- Cut 16 squares 2″ × 2″.

LARGE-SCALE TRIBAL PRINT
- Cut 4 rectangles 2″ × 3½″.
- Cut 1 square 3½″ × 3½″.

WHITE SOLID
- Cut 4 squares 2″ × 2″.

Construction

Note: All seam allowances are a scant ¼˝. See arrows on the illustrations for pressing direction.

1 | Use an aqua 2˝ square to add a triangle corner (page 119) to one end of each purple print 2˝ × 5˝ rectangle as shown, paying careful attention to the direction of the diagonal.

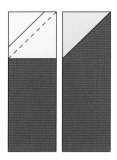

2 | Use an aqua square to add a triangle corner to one end of each purple print 2˝ × 3½˝ rectangle, this time with the diagonal slanted in the opposite direction as shown.

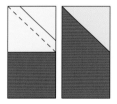

3 | Use a black print square, white square, black rectangle, and 1 each of the units from Steps 1 and 2 to assemble a corner unit as shown. Make 4.

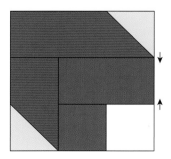

4 | Use 2 aqua squares and a medium-scale tribal print 2˝ × 3½˝ rectangle to make a Flying Geese unit (page 120). Make 4.

5 | Sew a unit from Step 5 between a medium-scale tribal print rectangle and a large-scale tribal print rectangle as shown. Make 4.

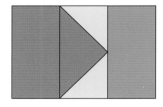

6 | Assemble the block as shown.

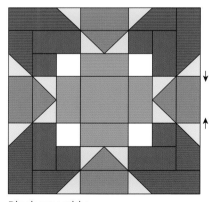

Block assembly

Sunburst

FINISHED BLOCK:
12″ × 12″

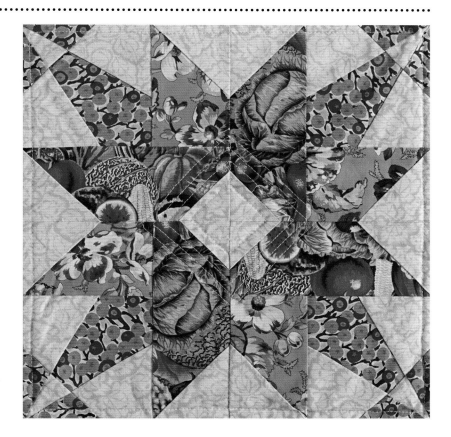

Block designed by Linda and Carl Sullivan with Snow Leopard Designs, sewn by Linda and Carl Sullivan

Fabric collection: FreeSpirit English Garden by Snow Leopard Designs

Technique: Foundation paper piecing

See this block in *Cozy* (page 108).

Ingredients

CREAM PRINT: ¼ yard

ORANGE PRINT: ¼ yard

RED LARGE-SCALE PRINT: ⅛ yard

BLUE LARGE-SCALE PRINT: ⅛ yard

8½″ × 11″ FOUNDATION PAPER:
Such as Carol Doak's Foundation Paper (by C&T Publishing)

SUNBURST FOUNDATION PATTERNS A AND B (pages 82 and 83): Make 4 copies of each pattern. (To download, see page 6.)

Cutting

CREAM PRINT

• Cut 16 rectangles 3″ × 4″ (2A, 3A, 6A, and 7A).

• Cut 4 rectangles 2½″ × 4″ (8A).

• Cut 4 rectangles 1½″ × 3″ (1B).

ORANGE PRINT

• Cut 4 rectangles 3″ × 4½″ (1A).

• Cut 8 rectangles 2″ × 3″ (2B and 3B).

RED LARGE-SCALE PRINT

• Cut 4 rectangles 3½″ × 7″ (5A).

BLUE LARGE-SCALE PRINT

• Cut 4 rectangles 3½″ × 4½″ (4A).

Construction

Note: All seam allowances are a scant ¼˝. Press each seam as it is sewn, using a dry iron.

1 | Refer to Foundation Paper Piecing (page 120) to piece the A and B foundations in order, matching the fabric in the cutting directions to the sections listed on the paper. Make 4 each of A and B.

2 | Trim the foundation triangles on the outside solid line.

3 | With the paper still attached, sew a foundation A unit to a foundation B unit. Make 4.

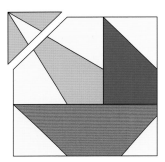

4 | Assemble the block as shown. Remove the papers in reverse order.

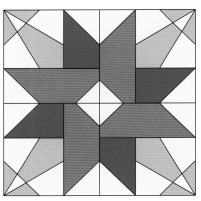

Block assembly

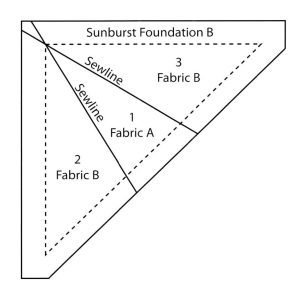

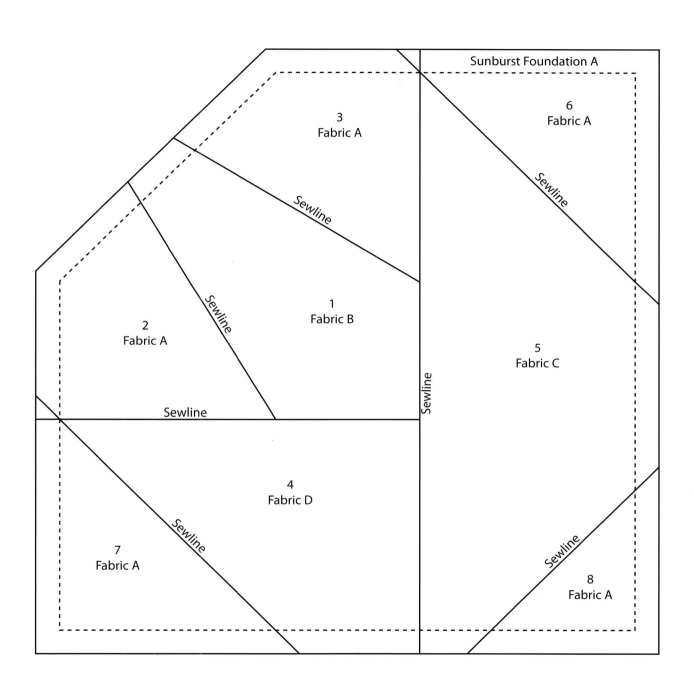

Sunburst Foundation A

3
Fabric A

6
Fabric A

Sewline

Sewline

1
Fabric B

Sewline

2
Fabric A

5
Fabric C

Sewline

Sewline

4
Fabric D

7
Fabric A

Sewline

8
Fabric A

Sewline

Compass

FINISHED BLOCK:
12″ × 12″

Block designed by Sharon Thornton with Kerri Thomson, sewn by Kerri Thomson

Fabric collection: FreeSpirit Washington Depot by Denyse Schmidt

Techniques: Piecing, foundation paper piecing

See this block in *Cozy* (page 108).

Ingredients

CREAM SOLID: ¼ yard

MEDIUM PINK FLORAL: 1 fat eighth

DARK PINK PRINT: ⅛ yard

COMPASS FOUNDATION PATTERN (next page): Make 4 copies of the pattern. (To download, see page 6.)

Cutting

CREAM SOLID

• Cut 8 rectangles 1¾″ × 6½″.

• Cut 16 squares 2¼″ × 2¼″.

MEDIUM PINK FLORAL

• Cut 20 squares 2¼″ × 2¼″.

DARK PINK PRINT

• Cut 4 rectangles 2½″ × 6¼″.

• Cut 1 square 2″ × 2″.

Construction

Note: All seam allowances are a scant ¼˝. See arrows on the illustrations for pressing direction.

1 | Sew the light and medium squares to form nine-patch units. Make 4.

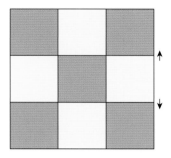

2 | Refer to Foundation Paper Piecing (page 120) to piece the foundation in order, using the dark pink print rectangle in the center and the cream solid rectangles on each side. Make 4.

3 | Trim the foundation triangles on the outside solid line, 2˝ × 5¾˝. Remove the papers in reverse order.

Piece 4 star points using paper foundation pattern.

4 | Assemble the block as shown.

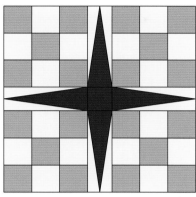

Block assembly

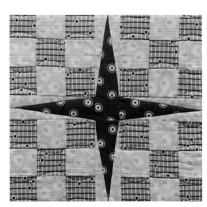

Alternate colorway for Compass (see block in *Over Here*, page 99)

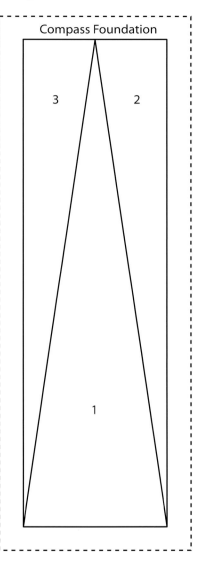

Compass Foundation

3 2

1

Prismatic

FINISHED BLOCK:
12″ × 12″

Block designed by Kerri Thomson with Sharon Thornton, sewn by Kerri Thomson

Fabric collection: FreeSpirit Floral Retrospective and FreeSpirit Loominous by Anna Maria Horner

Technique: Foundation paper piecing

See this block in *Subdivision* (page 100).

Ingredients

YELLOW ROSE PRINT: 1 square 6″ × 6″

SMALL FLORAL PRINT: ¼ yard

GRAY WOVEN: ¼ yard

PRISMATIC PATTERN (next page):
Make 1 copy of the pattern at 200%, or download the pattern in quadrants, print full-size, and tape them together. (To download, see page 6.)

Cutting

YELLOW ROSE PRINT

• Cut 1 square 5¾″ × 5¾″.

SMALL FLORAL PRINT

• Cut 8 squares 4¼″ × 4¼″.
  Subcut in half diagonally.

GRAY WOVEN

• Cut 4 rectangles 2¼″ × 6″.

• Cut 4 rectangles 2¼″ × 8½″.

• Cut 4 rectangles 2¼″ × 10¾″.

Construction

Press each seam as it is sewn, using a dry iron.

1 | Refer to Foundation Paper Piecing (page 120) to piece the block. Start at the center with the yellow rose print square, and add the small floral print triangles and gray woven rectangles in numerical order until the foundation is covered.

2 | Trim the block to 12½″ × 12½″. Remove the papers in reverse order.

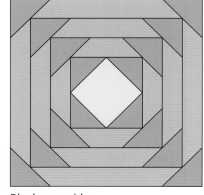

Block assembly

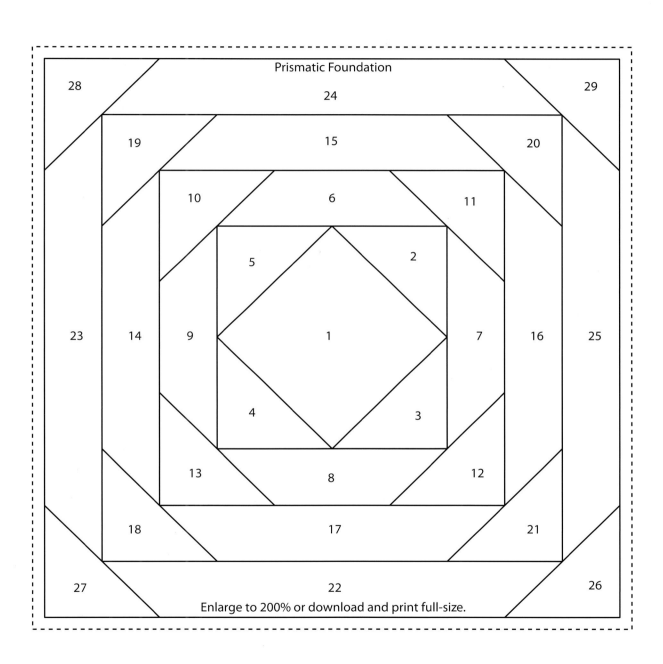

Prismatic Foundation

Enlarge to 200% or download and print full-size.

Windblown

FINISHED BLOCK: 12″ × 12″

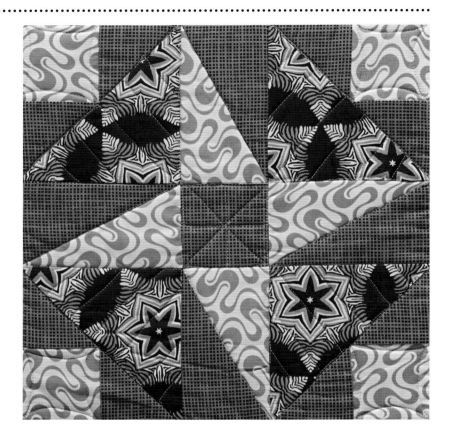

Block designed by Kerri Thomson with Sharon Thornton, sewn by Kerri Thomson

Fabric collection: FreeSpirit Hello Love by Heather Bailey

Technique: Piecing

See this block in *Over Here* (page 96).

Ingredients

BLUE STAR PRINT: 1 fat eighth

BLUE WAVY LINE PRINT: 1 fat eighth

BLUE TONE ON TONE: 1 fat eighth

TEMPLATE PLASTIC

WINDBLOWN STAR POINT PATTERN (next page): Make 1 copy of the pattern. (To download, see page 6.) Make a template for the star points.

Cutting

BLUE STAR PRINT

- Cut 2 squares 5⅝″ × 5⅝″. Subcut in half diagonally.

BLUE WAVY LINE PRINT

- Cut 4 squares 2⅞″ × 2⅞″.
- Cut 4 star points, using the template made from the pattern.

BLUE TONE ON TONE

- Cut 4 squares 3¼″ × 3¼″. Subcut in half diagonally.
- Cut 1 square 3″ × 3″.
- Cut 4 star points, using the template made from the pattern.

Construction

Note: All seam allowances are a scant ¼˝. See arrows on the illustrations for pressing direction.

1 | Sew 2 different star point triangles together. Make 4.

2 | Use a large blue star print triangle, 2 small blue tone-on-tone triangles, and 1 blue wavy line print square to assemble a corner unit as shown. Make 4.

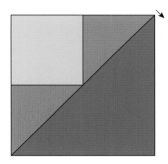

3 | Assemble the block as shown.

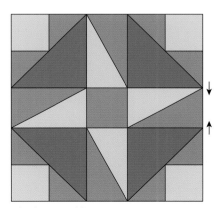

Block assembly

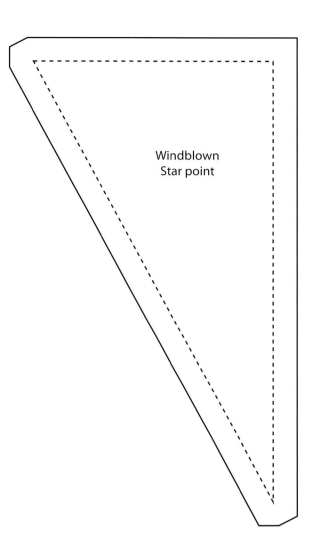

Windblown
Star point

Glamping

FINISHED BLOCK:
12″ × 12″

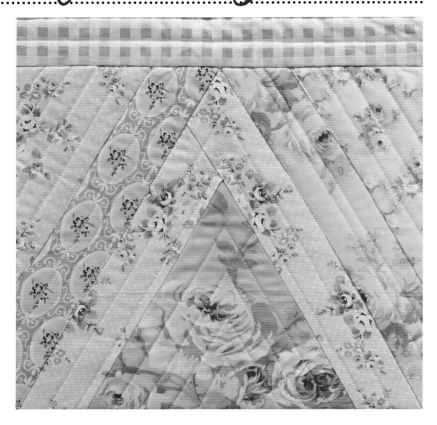

Block designed by Tanya Whelan,
sewn by Kerri Thomson

Fabric collection: FreeSpirit Charlotte
by Tanya Whelan

Technique: Foundation paper piecing

See this block in *Subdivision* (page 100).

Ingredients

GREEN LARGE ROSE PRINT: 1 fat quarter

PINK FLORAL PRINT: ¼ yard

GREEN FLORAL PRINT: 1 rectangle 3½″ × 16″

GREEN BLOSSOM DOT PRINT: 1 rectangle 3½″ × 16″

PINK FLORAL LATTICE PRINT: 1 rectangle 6″ × 11″

PINK GINGHAM PRINT: 1 rectangle 3½″ × 16″

GLAMPING FOUNDATION PATTERN (next page):
Make 1 copy of the pattern at 200%, or download
the pattern in quadrants, print full-size, and tape
them together. (To download, see page 6.)

Cutting

GREEN LARGE ROSE PRINT
- Cut 1 rectangle
  9″ × 10″ (#**1**).

PINK FLORAL PRINT
- Cut 1 rectangle
  5″ × 9½″ (#**6**).
- Cut 2 rectangles
  3″ × 13½″ (#**2** and #**3**).

GREEN FLORAL PRINT
- Cut 1 rectangle
  2¾″ × 14″ (#**4**).

GREEN BLOSSOM DOT PRINT
- Cut 1 rectangle
  2¾″ × 14″ (#**5**).

PINK FLORAL LATTICE PRINT
- Cut 1 rectangle
  5″ × 9½″ (#**7**).

PINK GINGHAM PRINT
- Cut 1 rectangle
  2¾″ × 13½″ (#**8**).

Construction

Press as each seam is sewn, using a dry iron.

1 | Refer to Foundation Paper Piecing (page 120) to piece the block in order, matching the fabrics listed in the cutting directions to the sections on the pattern.

2 | Trim the block to 12½″ × 12½″. Remove the papers in reverse order.

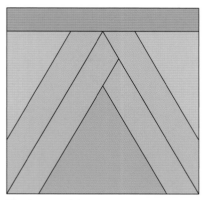

Block assembly

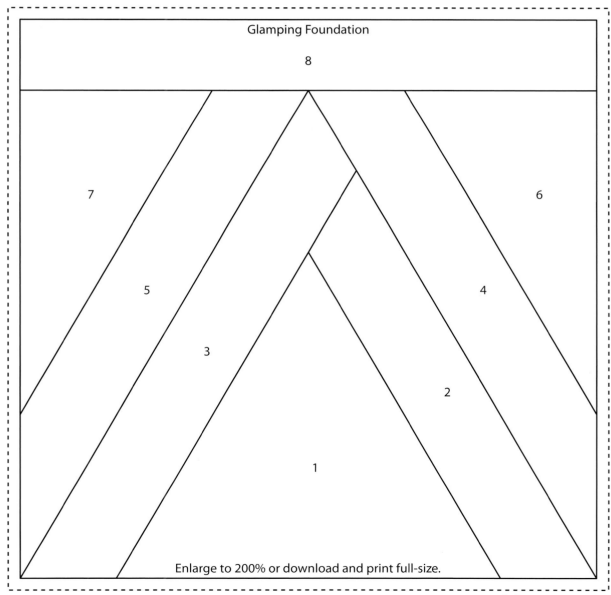

Glamping Foundation

8

7

6

5

4

3

2

1

Enlarge to 200% or download and print full-size.

Six Sides

FINISHED BLOCK:
12″ × 12″

Block designed by Tanya Whelan,
sewn by Kerri Thomson

Fabric collection: FreeSpirit Charlotte
by Tanya Whelan

Techniques: Piecing, appliqué, Y-seams

See this block in *Subdivision* (page 100).

Ingredients

PINK FLORAL PRINT: 1 square 10″ × 10″

GRAY FLORAL PRINT: 1 fat eighth

GREEN GINGHAM PRINT: 1 square 14″ × 14″

TEMPLATE PLASTIC

**SIX SIDES HEXAGON AND BORDER PATTERNS
(page 94):** Make 1 copy of each pattern.
(To download, see page 6.) Make plastic
templates.

Cutting

PINK FLORAL PRINT

• Cut 1 hexagon, using hexagon template.

GRAY FLORAL PRINT

• Cut 6 border pieces, using border template.

GREEN GINGHAM PRINT

• Cut 1 square 12½″ × 12½″.

Construction

Note: All seam allowances are a scant ¼˝. Press the seams as noted.

1 | Pin the center hexagon and 1 hexagon border piece right sides together, matching the edges. Stitch along the pinned edges, starting and stopping ¼˝ from the side edges. Press the seam toward the center hexagon.

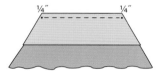

2 | Repeat Step 1 to add the remaining border pieces around the center hexagon.

3 | Fold the center hexagon in half, right sides together, along one of the points, matching the border piece side edges and pin. Starting at the outer edge, sew on the pinned edge, stopping at the seam with the center hexagon.

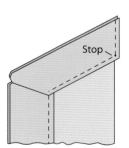

Sew borders together at each edge.

4 | Repeat Step 3 to sew the remaining border seams together. Press the border seams open.

5 | Press the outer border edge under ¼˝ and center the pieced hexagon on top of the background square, right side up. Use your favorite appliqué method to sew the outer edge of the hexagon to the background square.

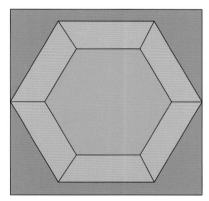

Block assembly

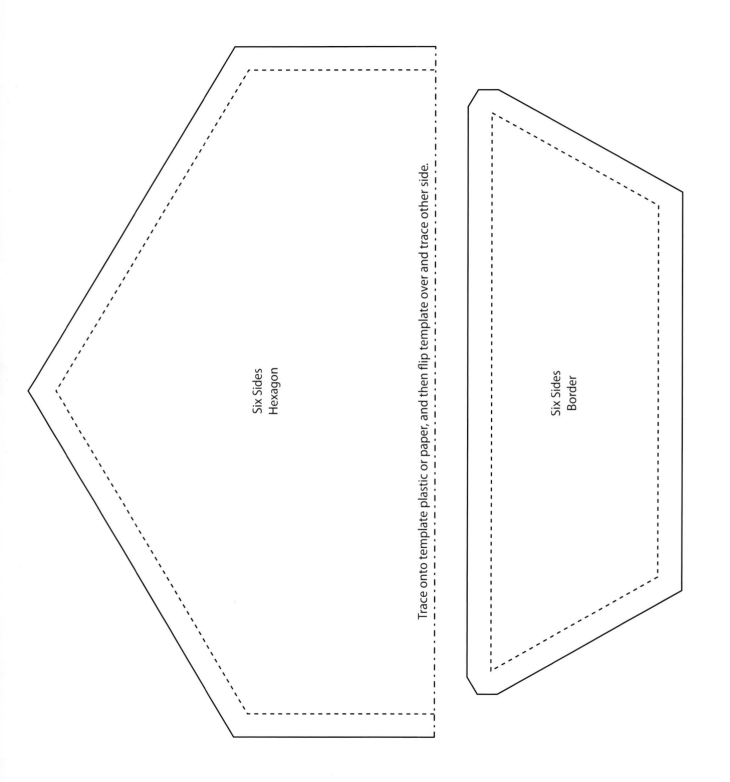

Six Sides
Hexagon

Trace onto template plastic or paper, and then flip template over and trace other side.

Six Sides
Border

Part 2:
Sampler Quilts

Turn your sampler blocks into a beautiful quilt you'll use for years to come! The five quilt projects that follow are designed to show off your quilt blocks in unexpected ways, with bold layouts and clean, modern lines.

Tips for Success:

- Group blocks of similar color stories into the same quilts or in the same area of a quilt.

- When arranging your quilt blocks, take a photo so you can review your favorite layouts.

- Choose background and accent fabric that complements the fabric prints you use in the blocks.

- Add neutral solids to your quilt for a serene feel, and add bold brights for a real wow factor. We used FreeSpirit Designer Essentials Solids.

Over Here

FINISHED QUILT:
67″ × 67″

Keep it simple, with a hint of the unexpected. A nine-block sampler quilt, this layout offers a great way to highlight blocks of the same color scheme. In this case, the blues and pinks play well off each other to create a harmonious color scheme, while the aqua background brings out the boldness of the cool tones.

Made by Lindsay Conner, quilted by Darcie Mair

Skill level: Beginner

Blocks featured: Boutonniere (page 8), Coronet (page 11), Diadem (page 14), Kaleidoscope* (page 36), Judith's Fan (page 55), Compass (page 84), Windblown (page 88)

Kaleidoscope is used three times in different colorways.

Ingredients

9 SAMPLER BLOCKS:
Trim size 12½″ × 12½″

AQUA SOLID: 2¾ yards

NAVY SOLID: ½ yard

BINDING: ⅔ yard

BACKING: 4¼ yards

BATTING: 75″ × 75″

Cutting

AQUA SOLID

• Cut 1 strip 12½″ × 41½″ for top border.

• Cut 1 strip 6½″ × 41½″ for inner bottom border.

• Cut 2 strips 7½″ × width of fabric. Piece to make 1 strip 7½″ × 59½″ for left border.

• Cut 2 strips 13½″ × width of fabric. Piece to make 1 strip 13½″ × 59½″ for inner right border. From leftovers, cut 6 strips 3″ × 12½″ for vertical sashing.

• Cut 2 strips 3″ × 41½″ for horizontal sashing.

• Cut 2 strips 5½″ × width of fabric. Piece to make 1 strip 5½″ × 59½″ for outer right border.

• Cut 2 strips 6″ × width of fabric. Piece to make 1 strip 6″ × 61½″ for outer bottom border. Subcut 1 rectangle 5½″ × 6″ for border corner square.

NAVY SOLID

• Cut 2 strips 3″ × width of fabric. Piece to make 1 strip 3″ × 66½″ for bottom accent border.

• Cut 2 strips 1½″ × width of fabric. Piece to make 1 strip 1½″ × 60½″ and 1 strip 1½″ × 6″ for vertical accent border.

BINDING FABRIC

• Cut 8 strips 2½″ × 40″ for double-fold binding.

Construction

Note: All seam allowances are a scant ¼˝. See arrows on the illustrations for pressing direction.

1 | Arrange the sampler blocks in 3 rows of 3. Place vertical sashing pieces between the blocks in the rows and sew together.

2 | Add horizontal sashing pieces between the rows.

3 | Sew the 12½˝ × 41½˝ top border and the 6½˝ × 41½˝ inner bottom border to the joined blocks.

4 | Sew the 7½˝ × 59½˝ left border and the 13½˝ × 59½˝ right border to the joined blocks.

5 | Add the 1½˝ × 59½˝ navy accent border and the 5½˝ × 59½˝ outer right border.

6 | Sew the 1½˝ × 6˝ navy rectangle and the 5½˝ × 6˝ border corner rectangle together to the bottom border and add to the quilt.

Quilting and Finishing

Layer, baste, quilt, and bind using your favorite methods. (For more information, go to ctpub.com, scroll down, and click Support: Quiltmaking Basics and Sewing Tips.)

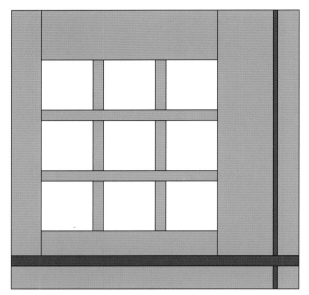

Quilt assembly

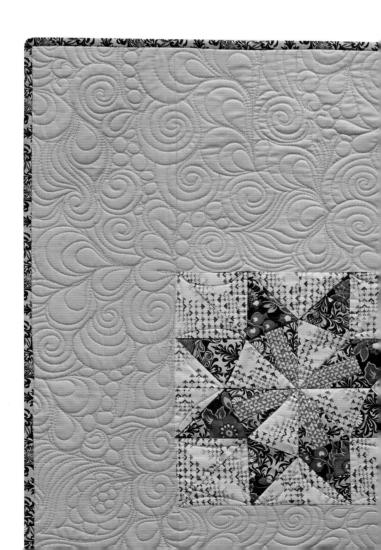

Subdivision

Arrange your sampler blocks into a quaint neighborhood of colored roads and refreshing symmetry. This 15-block sampler project makes a cozy lap quilt. With straightforward piecing, the top goes together in no time.

Made by Lindsay Conner, quilted by Darcie Mair

Skill level: Beginner

Blocks featured:
Corsage (page 20), On Target (page 23), Value Matters (page 28), Spooled (page 40), Orange Peel (page 42), Snowy Owl (page 45), Sunny Isle Butterflies (page 59), Spinwheel (page 68), Maltese (page 71), Five Spot (page 73), Snowbank (page 76), X Marks the Spot (page 77), Prismatic (page 86), Glamping (page 90), Six Sides (page 92)

Ingredients

15 SAMPLER BLOCKS:
Trim size 12½″ × 12½″

WHITE SOLID: 2⅜ yards

LIGHT BLUE SOLID: ⅛ yard

GREEN SOLID: ⅛ yard

NAVY SOLID: ⅛ yard

MAGENTA SOLID: ⅛ yard

BINDING: ⅔ yard

BACKING: 4¼ yards

BATTING: 72″ × 76″

Cutting

WHITE

- Cut 4 strips 1½″ × 34½″ for vertical sashing.

- Cut 8 strips 3″ × width of fabric. Piece to make 4 strips 3″ × 68½″ for outer vertical sashing.

- Cut 8 strips 4″ × width of fabric. Piece to make 4 strips 4″ × 68½″ for inner vertical sashing.

- Cut 4 strips 2½″ × width of fabric. Subcut 12 rectangles 2½″ × 12½″ for horizontal sashing.

LIGHT BLUE, GREEN, NAVY, AND MAGENTA

- Cut 1 strip 1½″ × 34½″ from each color for sashing accent strips.

BINDING

- Cut 8 strips 2½″ × 40″ for double-fold binding.

Construction

Note: All seam allowances are a scant ¼˝. See arrows on the illustrations for pressing direction.

1 | Arrange the blocks in 3 columns of 5. Place sashing rectangles between the blocks in each column and sew together.

2 | Pair the 1½˝ white strips with the sashing accent strips. Sew the ends together and press to the accent strips.

3 | Sew the 3˝ × 68½˝ vertical sashing strips to the sides of the light blue and magenta pieces. Sew the 4˝ × 68½˝ vertical sashing strips to the sides of the green and navy accent pieces.

4 | Arrange and sew the block columns and sashing pieces together.

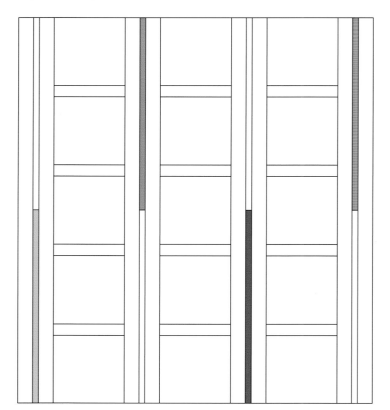

Quilt assembly

Quilting and Finishing

Layer, baste, quilt, and bind using your favorite methods. (For more information, go to ctpub.com, scroll down, and click Support: Quiltmaking Basics and Sewing Tips.)

Tribal

With placeholders for six assorted blocks, this modern take on a sampler quilt makes a bold statement. Best of all, the layout is easy enough for advanced beginners to tackle.

Made by Lindsay Conner

Skill level: Advanced beginner

Blocks featured: Arizona (page 21), Sunset (page 26), Melon Flower (page 34), Agape (page 48), London (page 52), Derailed (page 70),

Ingredients

6 SAMPLER BLOCKS:
Trim size 12½″ unfinished

BLUE SOLID: 1⅛ yards

GOLD SOLID: ½ yard

RED SOLID: ⅜ yard

BINDING: ½ yard

BACKING: 3⅛ yards

BATTING: 58″ × 56″

Cutting

BLUE

- Cut 3 strips 4″ × width of fabric. Piece to make 2 strips 4″ × 48½″ for vertical sashing.

- Cut 2 strips 8½″ × 24½″ for triangle borders.

- Cut 3 squares 8⅞″ × 8⅞″ for half-square triangles.

- Cut 8 rectangles 3½″ × 4½″ for pieced horizontal sashing.

GOLD

- Cut 3 squares 8⅞″ × 8⅞″ for half-square triangles.

- Cut 8 rectangles 3½″ × 4½″ for pieced horizontal sashing.

RED

- Cut 2 strips 3½″ × width of fabric. Piece to make 1 strip 3½″ × 48½″ for vertical sashing.

- Cut 8 rectangles 3½″ × 4½″ for pieced horizontal sashing.

BINDING

- Cut 6 strips 2½″ × 40″ for double-fold binding.

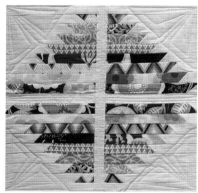

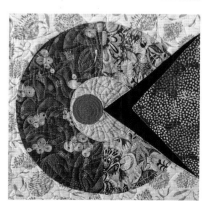

Construction

Note: All seam allowances are a scant ¼˝. See arrows on the illustrations for pressing direction.

1 | Using the blue and gold 8⅞˝ squares, make 6 half-square triangles (page 119).

2 | Sew the half-square triangles together into 2 columns of 3 blocks each. Sew to the 8¼˝ × 24½˝ border pieces. Add the 4˝ × 48½˝ vertical sashing pieces to the borders as shown.

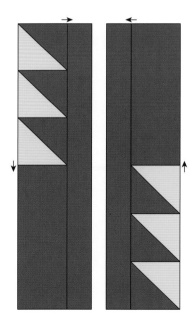

3 | Sew the blue, gold, and red 3½˝ × 4½˝ rectangles together to make the pieced horizontal sashing. Make 8.

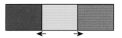

4 | Sew the pieced sashing and blocks together in 2 columns of 3 blocks each.

5 | Sew the red 3½˝ × 48½˝ red sashing strip between the columns.

6 | Add the triangle borders.

Quilt assembly

Quilting and Finishing

Layer, baste, quilt, and bind using your favorite methods. (For more information, go to ctpub.com, scroll down, and click Support: Quiltmaking Basics and Sewing Tips.)

Cozy

Soft colors and a simple, surprising layout make this decorative quilt a welcome home for your sampler blocks. Show them off by framing each block in a color that brings out its beauty, with a geometric background to tie them together.

Made by Lindsay Conner

Skill level: Intermediate

Blocks featured: Solitaire (page 9), Collage Basket (page 32), Sunburst (page 81), Compass (page 84)

Ingredients

4 SAMPLER BLOCKS: Trim size 12½″ × 12½″

WHITE SOLID: 2 yards

CREAM PRINT: 1½ yards

RED, ORANGE, YELLOW, AND TAN SOLIDS: ¼ yard each

BINDING: ⅝ yard

BACKING: 3½ yards

BATTING: 63″ × 63″

Cutting

WHITE

- Cut 1 strip 3½″ × width of fabric. Subcut 4 rectangles 3½″ × 5½″ for block sashing centers.

- Cut 16 squares 2″ × 2″ for arrow points.

- Cut 3 strips 10½″ × width of fabric. Subcut 2 rectangles 10½″ × 28″, 2 rectangles 10½″ × 11½″, and 2 rectangles 10½″ × 16″ for pieced top and bottom borders.

- Cut 2 more strips 10½″ × width of fabric. Subcut 2 rectangles 10½″ × 18″, 2 rectangles 10½″ × 16″, and 2 squares 1½″ × 1½″ for pieced side borders.

CREAM PRINT

- Cut 1 strip 3½″ × width of fabric. Subcut 4 rectangles 3½″ × 5½″ for block sashings and 1 piece 3½″ × 3½″ for quilt center.

- Cut 2 strips 10½″ × width of fabric. Subcut 2 rectangles 10½″ × 21½″ for pieced top and bottom borders, 2 rectangles 10½″ × 12½″ for pieced border sides, and 2 squares 7″ × 7″ for pieced borders. (Tip: Cut 1 of each from each strip.)

- Cut 2 strips 7″ × width of fabric. Subcut 6 additional squares 7″ × 7″ for pieced borders and 4 rectangles 7″ × 3½″ for block sashing.

RED, ORANGE, YELLOW, AND TAN
From each color:

- Cut 2 strips 2½″ × 12½″ for block frames.

- Cut 2 strips 2½″ × 16½″ for block frames.

BINDING

- Cut 7 strips 2½″ × 40″ for double-fold binding.

Construction

Note: All seam allowances are a scant ¼″. See arrows on the illustrations for pressing direction.

Quilt Center

1 | Arrange the sampler blocks in 2 rows of 2. Pair each block with a complementary set of framing strips.

2 | Sew the 12½″ framing strips to the sides. Sew the 16½″ strips to the top and the bottom.

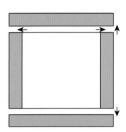

3 | Using the white 2″ squares, make triangle corners (page 119) on 2 corners of a short side of each 3½″ × 7″ cream rectangle.

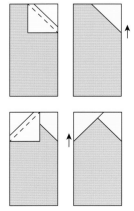

4 | Repeat Step 3 to make triangle corners on a short end of each 3½″ × 5″ rectangle.

5 | Sew a white 3½″ × 5½″ rectangle between the units from Steps 3 and 4 as shown. Make 4.

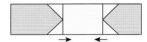

6 | Referring to the quilt assembly diagram (page 113), sew 2 sashing units between the blocks. Sew the cream 3½″ square between the remaining sashing units. Join the rows.

Side Borders

1 | Use cream 7″ squares to make a triangle corner (page 119) on the top left corner of 2 white 10½″ × 18″ side border rectangles.

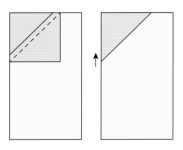

2 | Use cream 7″ squares to make a triangle corner on the top right corner of 2 white 10½″ × 16″ side border rectangles.

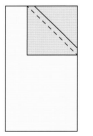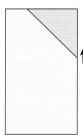

3 | Use white 1½″ squares to make a triangle corner on the top right corner of 2 cream 10½″ × 12½″ side border rectangles.

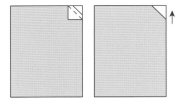

4 | Place the unit from Step 2 and the unit from Step 3 perpendicularly as shown. Draw a diagonal line across the overlapped corner. Sew on the line. Trim ¼″ past the seam. Make 2.

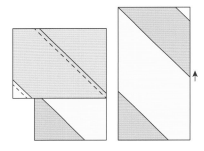

5 | Arrange the side border units on each side of the quilt center so that the cream corners meet in the center as shown in the quilt assembly diagram. Sew to the quilt center.

Top and Bottom Borders

1 | Use a cream 7″ square to make a triangle corner on the top right corner of 2 white 10½″ × 28″ top and bottom border rectangles.

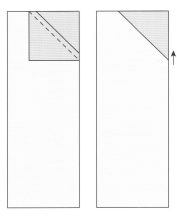

2 | Use a cream 7″ square to make a triangle corner on the top left corner of 2 white 10½″ × 16″ top and bottom border rectangles.

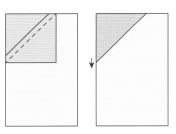

3 | Place a cream 10½″ × 21½″ top and bottom border rectangle and the unit from Step 2 together perpendicularly as shown. Draw a line across the overlapped corner. Sew on the line. Trim ¼″ past the seam. Make 2.

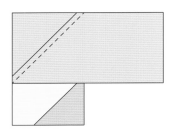

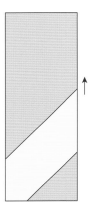

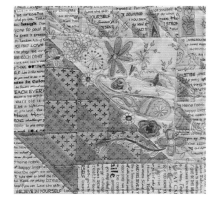

4 | Place a white 10½″ × 11½″ top and bottom border rectangle and the unit from Step 3 together perpendicularly as shown. Sew together diagonally as described in Step 3.

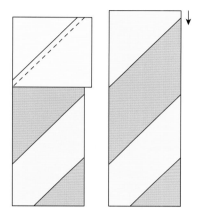

5 | Arrange the top and bottom border units on the top and bottom of the quilt center so that the cream corners meet in the center as shown in the quilt assembly diagram. Sew to the quilt center.

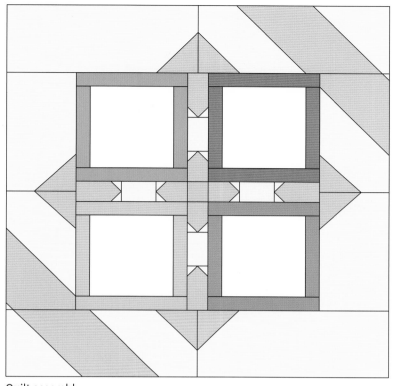

Quilt assembly

Quilting and Finishing

Layer, baste, quilt, and bind using your favorite methods. (For more information, go to ctpub.com, scroll down, and click Support: Quiltmaking Basics and Sewing Tips.)

Neighbors

FINISHED QUILT:
54˝ × 80˝

Welcome to the neighborhood! Sew a nine-block sampler of modern blocks, tying together cool colors with complementary solids. A bold layout, this double-size quilt can easily be extended 4˝ on the sides to make it queen size.

Made by Lindsay Conner, quilted by Darcie Mair

Skill level: Intermediate

Blocks featured: Revolution (page 17), Star Popper (page 27), Spun (page 31), Askew (page 38), Fly Away (page 62), Tidepool (page 63), Wildwood (page 64), Mod Cabin (page 65), Four Points (page 79)

Ingredients

9 SAMPLER BLOCKS:
Trim size 12½˝ × 12½˝

PURPLE: 3½ yards

LIME: ½ yard

NAVY: ⅜ yard

TEAL: ¼ yard

BINDING: ⅔ yard

BACKING: 5 yards

BATTING: 62˝ × 88˝

FUSIBLE WEB: ½ yard

Cutting

PURPLE

• Cut 1 strip 5˝ × width of fabric. Subcut 4 rectangles 5˝ × 7⅜˝ for rooftop background pieces. *Subcut 2 rectangles in half diagonally between the top left and bottom right corners; subcut the remaining 2 in half diagonally in the opposite direction.*

• Cut 4 strips 3½˝ × width of fabric. Subcut 10 rectangles 3½˝ × 12½˝ for horizontal sashing.

• Cut 2 strips 2½˝ × width of fabric. Subcut 4 rectangles 2½˝ × 12½˝ for narrow horizontal sashing.

• Cut 4 strips 5½˝ × width of fabric. Piece to make 2 strips 5½˝ × 60½˝ for outer vertical sashing.

• Cut 4 strips 4½˝ × width of fabric. Piece to make 2 strips 4½˝ × 60½˝ for inner vertical sashing.

• Cut 2 strips 8½˝ × width of fabric. Piece to make 1 strip 8½˝ × 54½˝ for top border.

• Cut 2 strips 6½˝ × width of fabric. Piece to make 1 strip 6½˝ × 54½˝ for bottom border.

• Cut 2 rectangles 9½˝ × 12½˝ for bottom block sashing.

LIME

• Cut 2 strips 4⅝˝ × width of fabric. Subcut 4 rectangles 4⅝˝ × 13⅝˝ for rooftops. *Fold each in half along the 13⅝˝ side and mark the center; draw a line from the top center point down to each bottom corner. Trim off the triangle corners, cutting on the lines you've drawn.*

• Cut 2 strips 2½˝ × width of fabric. Piece to make 1 strip 2½˝ × 54½˝ for top border.

NAVY

• Cut 2 strips 4½˝ × width of fabric. Piece to make 1 strip 4½˝ × 54½˝ for bottom border.

TEAL

• Cut 1 strip 4½˝ × width of fabric. Subcut 5 pieces 4½˝ × 6½˝ for triangle appliqués. *Fold in half along the 6½˝ side and mark the center; draw a line from the top center fold down to each bottom corner. Trim off the triangle corners, cutting on the lines you've drawn.*

BINDING

• Cut 8 strips 2½˝ × 40˝ for double-fold binding.

Construction

Note: All seam allowances are a scant ¼˝. See arrows on the illustrations for pressing direction.

1 | Piece the rooftops from the purple and lime triangles. Start by placing a left purple corner triangle on a lime base triangle. Place the purple triangle about ¼˝ from the base of the lime triangle and sew a scant ¼˝ from the edge, making sure to leave ½˝ of purple fabric extending off the opposite end. Add the other purple triangle. Trim the pieces to 12½˝ × 4½˝.

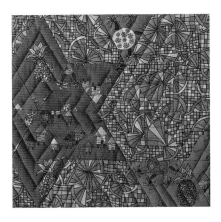

2 | Arrange the sampler blocks, sashing pieces, and rooftops in 3 columns as shown.

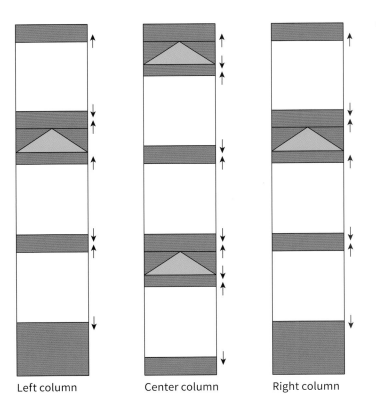

Left column   Center column   Right column

- Sew the 2½˝ horizontal sashing rectangles between 4 blocks and the rooftop pieces above them.

- Sew the 9½˝ bottom block sashing rectangles below the last block on the left and right columns.

- Sew the 3½˝ horizontal sashing rectangles above and below the rest of the blocks and rooftop pieces.

3 | Sew together the columns, making sure to stay within the ¼˝ seam allowance so you do not sew over the rooftop points.

4 | Sew the 5½˝ outer vertical sashing strips to the outer edges of the left and right columns. Sew the 4½˝ inner vertical sashing strips between the columns.

5 | Sew the 2½˝ × 54½˝ lime border strip to the top of the quilt and the 4½˝ × 54½˝ navy border strip to the bottom of the quilt.

6 | Sew the 8½˝ × 54½˝ top border and the 6½˝ × 54½˝ bottom border to the quilt.

7 | Following the manufacturer's directions, fuse the teal triangles in place.

Quilting and Finishing

Layer, baste, quilt, and bind using your favorite methods. (For more information, go to ctpub.com, scroll down, and click Support: Quiltmaking Basics and Sewing Tips.)

Quilt assembly

Quiltmaking Techniques

Half-Square Triangles

Start with 2 squares of equal size. The size will be in the block instructions.

1 | With right sides together, pair 2 squares. Lightly draw a diagonal line from one corner to the opposite corner on the wrong side of 1 square.

Draw line.

2 | Sew a scant ¼″ seam on each side of the line.

Sew.

3 | Cut on the drawn line.

4 | Press, and trim off the dog-ears.

Triangle Corners

Start with a larger square or rectangle and 1, 2, 3, or 4 squares for the corners. The sizes will be in the block instructions.

1 | Lightly draw a diagonal line from one corner to the opposite corner on the wrong side of a corner square.

2 | With right sides together, place the square on one corner of a rectangle or bigger square, matching the direction of the square's diagonal line with the direction of the triangle you want to add to the corner. Sew directly on the line, trim the seam allowance to ¼″, and press to the corner.

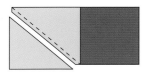

It's important to pay attention to the direction you want the triangle to be oriented.

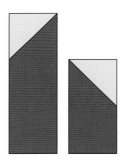

3 | If you want to add triangle corners to any of the remaining corners of the square or rectangle, repeat Steps 1 and 2.

4 | Starting with a large square, you can add triangle corners to 2 adjacent sides, 3 sides, or all 4 sides. If you make triangle

corners on all 4 corners, the result will be different depending on the relationship between the size of the larger and smaller squares.

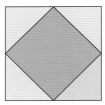

Square-in-a-Square block

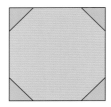

Snowball block

Flying Geese

Start with 1 rectangle and 2 squares. The sizes will be in the block instructions.

1 | Flying Geese are a specific type of triangle corner. Start by following Triangle Corners (page 119), Steps 1 and 2.

2 | Repeat on the other side of the rectangle with the second square.

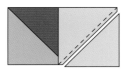

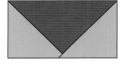

Foundation Paper Piecing

1 | Print out the foundation paper pattern at the correct scale. You may print onto regular computer paper or foundation paper for quilting, which tears off more easily after completing the block.

2 | Start with the piece of fabric for the first numbered section. Place the wrong side of the fabric on the wrong side of the paper pattern. Use a single pin or small dab of glue stick to adhere in place, making sure the entire section is covered.

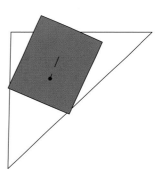

3 | Fold the paper back on the solid line between sections 1 and 2. Trim the first fabric's seam allowance to ¼″ and unfold the paper.

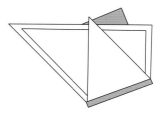

4 | Arrange the next piece of fabric (for section 2) right side down so that it matches the trimmed seam allowance of the first rectangle. Pin in place.

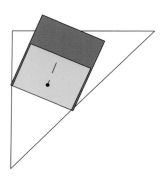

5 | Shorten your stitch length to secure your stitches and make it easier to tear off the paper later. From the printed side of the foundation paper, sew through all paper and fabric layers on the solid line between sections 1 and 2.

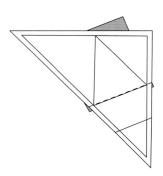

6 | Press the second fabric down towards section 3. Fold the paper back on the solid line between sections 2 and 3, and trim the seam allowance to ¼″. Unfold the paper.

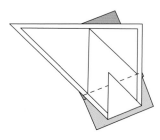

7 | Using all the remaining fabric pieces, finish sewing each section in numbered order in the same way.

8 | Leave the foundation papers on each section while joining together all of the parts of a block. After sewing the block together, carefully remove the papers.

Needle-Turn Appliqué

Place a few small appliqué pins to hold the shape in position. Use the tip of the needle to turn under the edges and stitch using a blind-hem stitch. It is best to pin and sew one shape at a time. Then continue adding shapes one at a time.

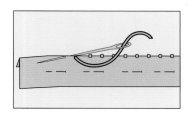

About the Designers

Photo by Isaac Bailey

Photo by David Butler

Photo by Lisa Fishbein

Photo by Joel Dewberry

HEATHER BAILEY
With sophisticated floral and geometric prints, Heather Bailey has inspired a new generation to embrace art and color in their everyday lives.
heatherbailey.com

AMY BUTLER has been making things all her life. One of her core beliefs is that through whom we are and what we do, we can inspire great change in ourselves, each other, and in the world.
amybutlerdesign.com

DENA DESIGNS is a hugely successful company that encompasses a wide array of products, ranging from home decor and accessories to greeting cards, gifts, craft items, books, and more.
denadesigns.com

JOEL DEWBERRY has an appreciation and love of all things tactile. Joel's sense of harmonizing an eclectic mix of design styles into a cohesive collection delivers a modern yet timeless style.
joeldewberry.com